The New Way of Jesus

The New Way of Jesus

Essays Presented to Howard Charles

Editor: William Klassen

Unless otherwise noted, all quotations from the Bible are from the Revised Standard Version
Old Testament Section, copyright 1952
New Testament Section, First Edition, copyright 1946
New Testament Section, Second Edition, © 1972
by Division of Christian Education of the National Council of Churches of Christ in the U.S.A.

Library of Congress Number 80-65049
International Standard Book Number 0-87303-038-9
Printed in the United States of America
Copyright © 1980 by Faith and Life Press
718B Main Street, Newton, Kansas 67114

This publication may not be reproduced, stored in a retrieval system, or transmitted in whole or in part, in any form or by any means, electronic, mechanical, photocopying, recording, or otherwise, without the prior written permission of Faith and Life Press.

Design by John Hiebert
Printing by Mennonite Press, Inc.

Contributors

Clarence Bauman
Associated Mennonite Biblical Seminaries

Jacob Elias
Associated Mennonite Biblical Seminaries

J. J. Enz
Associated Mennonite Biblical Seminaries

J. Massyngberde Ford
Notre Dame University

William Klassen
St. John's College, University of Manitoba

Millard Lind
Associated Mennonite Biblical Seminaries

John W. Miller
Conrad Grebel College, University of Waterloo, Ontario

Willard Swartley
Associated Mennonite Biblical Seminaries

J. C. Wenger
Associated Mennonite Biblical Seminaries

John H. Yoder
Notre Dame University
Associated Mennonite Seminaries

Preface

Howard Charles is a household name among Mennonites. To be sure, he may not be equally well known among all groups of Mennonites but his impact upon the Mennonite church as a whole has been very significant. His writings have strengthened the intellectual teaching level in Mennonite Sunday schools over many years. For forty years he has taught the New Testament to college students and seminarians from many lands.

When the idea of publishing a volume in his honor was first born, it was nurtured and kept alive by everyone who came in contact with it. I wish to express my gratitude for the encouragement given to the idea by J. J. Enz, Millard Lind, and John Howard Yoder. Our thanks to Howard and Miriam Charles for making available the text of a talk first given at the Associated Mennonite Biblical Seminaries in a series not intended for publication.

Editorial changes have been kept to a minimum. Standardization has been attempted, but for the most part each of Howard Charles's colleagues is here allowed to speak as he or she is accustomed. We know that as Howard reads these essays, his pencil will be very busy, for it is his custom to use his pencil freely on books he reads. He will find matters here that he agrees with. He will also raise questions at various points, and we hope that the reader is nudged beyond a previous understanding of the biblical text.

These essays will honor the scholarly teaching tradition of Howard Charles if they not only confirm the importance of the gospel, but also raise questions and challenge the reader to take another look at the text. Isaiah speaks of the new thing which Yahweh does, the way which is made even through the wilderness (43:18ff.). In that vast landscape known as *biblical studies*, which has seemed a wasteland or a wilderness to many, Howard Charles also keeps finding new paths, and through them brings many refreshing and liberating insights.

A word of appreciation is due Lorena Reimer who typed most of the manuscript; and above all, to Linda Block whose consummate skill as a typist, and patience as our departmental secretary, eased the burden of preparing this manuscript for publication. The University of Manitoba, through its Research Board has generously provided support for proofreading, typing, and the preparation of an index by Patty Hildebrand. The support of the Hesston Foundation and the Schowalter Foundation, both of whom provided us with a publishing subsidy, is gratefully acknowledged. Nevertheless, as every reader knows, the editor assumes responsibility for the shape of the volume and for all its shortcomings. Abbreviations used throughout follow the *Interpreter's Dictionary of the Bible*.

October 20, 1979

William Klassen
University of Manitoba
Winnipeg, Canada

Contents

Preface vii

J. C. Wenger
Howard Charles: An Appreciation 1

Howard Charles
My Spiritual Pilgrimage 7

Millard Lind
The Anomaly of the Prophet 17

Jacob J. Enz
The After life of the Ninth Plague (Darkness) in
    Bilbical Literature................................29

Josephine M. Ford
Three Ancient Jewish Views of Poverty 39

John W. Miller
Jesus' Personality as Reflected in His Parables........... 56

Willard M. Swartley
The Structural Function of the Term 'Way' in Mark....... 73

Jacob W. Elias
The Furious Climax in Nazareth (Luke 4:28-30)........... 87

William Klassen
The Novel Element in the Love Commandment of Jesus ... 100

John Howard Yoder
The Apostle's Apology Revisited 115

C. Bauman
Manifestations of the Spirit of God or Charismatic
    Movement 135

Index..148

Howard and Miriam Charles

1

Howard Charles: An Appreciation

J. C. Wenger

The Karli family is an old Bernese Mennonite family. One Peter Karli, for example, was banned from the land on June 23, 1651, as a member of the disobedient *Täufer* sect, one who persevered in that faith in a stiff-necked manner. The Karli immigrant to Pennsylvania was Henry, who arrived in 1737. Among the outstanding leaders of the Karli family (anglicized as Charles in America) may be mentioned John D. Charles, pastor of the Kansas City Mission Church, 1906-09, prominent member of the Hesston College faculty from the first, and dean and registrar there at his early death in 1923. John K. Charles was ordained minister at the Habeckers Congregation of the Lancaster Conference in 1913, and bishop five years later. H. Raymond Charles was ordained minister in 1941, and bishop in 1964, and has long served as a leader in the mission board of the Lancaster Mennonites.

Howard Hess Charles was born at Lititz, Pennsylvania, July 19, 1915, the son of Christian L. Charles and Ellen F. (Hess)—now in the tenth decade of her life. Soundly converted, he was active as a young man in the Christian education program of his congregation (Lititz) and district. He served both as a Sunday school teacher and superintendent, as a summer Bible school teacher and superintendent, as editor of the Lancaster Conference periodical, *The Missionary Messenger,* as a member of the Tract Committee of the Mennonite Publication Board, and as an employee of the Weaver (now Provident) Bookstore. A new chapter began in his life on July 15, 1943, when Bishop Amos S. Horst ordained him to the ministry of the Lititz congregation, four days short of twenty-eight years of age. In that church he served faithfully and effectively for four years.

Howard Charles has a good educational foundation. He

graduated from the advanced Bible course, Eastern Mennonite College, Virginia, in 1935. In 1940 Goshen College conferred on him the degree, Bachelor of Theology, and the next year, the B.A. In 1944 Union Theological Seminary in Virginia awarded him the Bachelor of Divinity degree, Princeton Seminary followed with a Master of Theology degree in 1948, and the University of Edinburgh in Scotland conferred the Ph.D. degree on him in 1958. His doctoral dissertation was entitled "The Charismatic Life in the Apostolic Church."

He began teaching in the Biblical Seminary of Goshen College in 1947, moved with the school to the Elkhart campus in 1969, and has served since 1958 on the faculty of the Associated Mennonite Biblical Seminaries, now located at Elkhart, Indiana. Charles has been active all through the years, broadening both his educational and church experience. He was a Fellow at Oxford University, 1965-66; he was engaged in a teaching mission in the Japanese Mennonite Church, 1961-62; and in a similar assignment in West Africa, 1973-74. In June 1979 it will be thirty-two years since he joined the Goshen Biblical Seminary faculty. Among his published works are: *Alcohol and the Bible,* 1966; *God and His People,* 1969; and a long list of essays for Mennonite Publishing House (Scottdale, Pa.) Sunday school materials. These materials have been received with much appreciation by the church.

On July 19, 1947, Howard was united in marriage to a Goshen College teacher, Miriam Stalter, of Elida, Ohio. They are the parents of two sons: J. Robert (1951) and Thomas E. (1960); both of whom are members of the church of their parents.

If one were to ask what has made Howard H. Charles the effective teacher he is, seven major characteristics could be mentioned.

First of all, Howard is outstanding for the clarity with which he is able to discuss a word, sentence, paragraph or section—even an overall view of a book. To listen to him teach New Testament studies is a delight. His preparation and meditation are so thorough that when he stands before a class he has much more material than he has time for. He has to select the very best and richest material to share with his students. And the students know that when they come to class they are going to be challenged, stimulated, forced to think, and compelled to produce sound results in solid Bible study. It is always a rich experience for students to sit at the feet of a mentor who can point the way to a grasp of the material at hand because he himself has thought through the issues and is able to present the material with such clarity that the truth on the pages of Scripture leaps into sharp focus. With Charles there is no hiding behind technical jargon. One can look into deep water because it is clear.

Second, the teaching and writing of Howard Charles are characterized by academic thoroughness. He has learned not to attempt to do more than he is able to do well. So there is little danger that a question of a student will catch him unprepared or will be one that he has not thought through. He prepares long and well for his classes and for his essays, and can take reasonable satisfaction in them. For he has studied until the deeper issues were crystal clear, and he is eager to share them with his students and readers. I recall asking him on one occasion why our Lord can be spoken of as the *Firstborn* of God's creation (Col. 1:15). His answer was quick, immediate, and satisfying. He explained that *Firstborn* has to do with status: that Christ is the preeminent one. (It is not that Christ was temporally older than the creation, but that he is the one who is over the whole creation: in fact, he is the one who brought the whole creation into being. Everything was created by him. And in a special sense, he is the Head of the Church, the body of those who have yielded to him, making him their Savior and Lord.) The whole context of Colossians 1:15-20 supports clearly the explanation which Charles had at the tip of his tongue.

Third, Howard Charles has demonstrated a willingness to face the more difficult questions encountered in the study of biblical books. Does the style of the pastoral Epistles differ from those of Paul's prison Epistles? If so, why? Does the style of 2 Peter differ, and in what ways, from the style of 1 Peter? How can one unravel the complex relationships of Matthew, Mark, and Luke? What was the common source from which Matthew and Luke drew, in addition to incorporating so much of Mark's Gospel? And how do the unique sections of Matthew and Luke differ from one another? Further, what was the organizing principle, the basic approach, of the Fourth Gospel? What sort of date should be assigned to the book of Hebrews? Does the book assume that the Jewish priests were still offering animal sacrifices—so that it was written before the fall of Jerusalem and the destruction of the temple in A.D. 70 by Titus? Such questions of authorship, sources, date, and style, where biblical scholars differ so sharply, provide the penetrating mind of a thorough scholar an opportunity to exercise a stabilizing influence on sincere seekers for the truth. Under a painting of the late Robert Dick Wilson of Princeton and Westminster Theological Seminaries, the caption stands: "I have not shirked the difficult questions." And that is precisely the tribute which the students of Howard H. Charles are able to give to him. Like C. H. Dodd, he believes that the path to truth goes *through* the critical question, not around it.

Fourth, Howard Charles knows how to make students work. They do not come to class hoping to soak up a bit of new information like a sponge absorbs water. They go from each class knowing what they are expected to do in preparation for the next one. They are expected to study, to organize, to produce. And they know that the professor will not be satisfied with shoddy work, with "pious" and glib answers which make a flimsy cover for poor preparation. Charles was himself a student of Howard T. Kuist, one of the very best guides to inductive Bible study, and he is able to assist students who are willing to work, to master this method of Bible study—making Bible study an ever richer experience, a fruitful source of sermons and teaching which feeds hearers with the rich meat of the Word.

Fifth, those who sit in his classes or associate with him otherwise, know that in this quiet and serious student there is also a restrained but keen wit, a delightful sense of humor. It is precisely this sense of good proportion which helps to make his lectures and sermons a delight to hear. It is not a matter of telling old stories over and over; it is much more the occasional flash of humor which enlivens the discussion and reveals a mind which is able to see that which is amusing in what might otherwise be a dull point.

Sixth, I think that it is permissible for a friend and colleague to report that Howard Charles is a man of deep humility, with an awareness that it is Christ who is to be glorified. It is the task of the instructor to help students see how great the Lord Jesus is, not how clever the instructor. This has nothing to do with the joy of creative scholarship, nor the satisfaction of a class period which seemed to be a blessing to the students. It is rather that attitude which does not measure success in terms of human recognition or praise, but which finds deep joy in helping others see something of the love, compassion, holiness, and sufficiency of the Savior. One's eye is on the Lord, and not on self. Along with all other true servants of Christ, Howard Charles knows that in himself he is nothing, but that Christ by his Spirit can use his servant to bring glory to the Lord of lords and King of kings. As his friends know, it is the desire of Howard Charles to be able to put at the end of each lecture, sermon, or essay: *Soli Deo Gloria!*

Finally, the greatest strength of Howard H. Charles must be mentioned. He is unashamedly a Christian believer. For him there is no question about who the Creator is—for God created all things, visible and invisible, through his Son, through his WORD; that Word which became flesh and tabernacled among us; that one who was as human as we are, yet who was also God incognito: paradoxically as human as we and also as divine as the Father. It was that eternal Son who, according to the flesh, was of the seed of David and heir of David's throne, who humbled himself and became obedient unto death, even the death of the cross. He is the one who was also the express image of the Father, the one who showed to mankind exactly what kind of person God really is. The New Testament does not follow the pattern of the Apostles' Creed, leaping from the birth of the Savior to his atoning death. Rather, it portrays for us that pattern of life which every true *Nachfolger* ("follower" or "disciple") shall live: a life of love, of holiness, of costly discipleship, of seeking to do good, not living to lay up treasures on earth, but in heaven. He who would follow the Savior must follow his Lord in taking up his individual cross of what it costs to do the will of God.

It is the representation of the New Testament that Christians are co-crucified with Christ, that they co-die with him, co-rise with him, co-ascend with him, and are co-seated with him on his throne in the "heavenlies." And this ascended Lord, who has the highest possible status both in this world and in that which is to come, baptizes each convert with the Holy Spirit, making him a partaker of the divine nature, and endowing him with both the fruit and gifts of the Spirit—such gifts as he can best utilize for the glory of the Lord and the upbuilding of his Body, the Church.

Although the Church Militant must face "the reproach of Christ," and sometimes drink of his awful cup, yet it can also look forward in joyous hope to his blessed return for his Bride—and the following Marriage Supper of the Lamb. When the last book of the New Testament canon reaches this scene there is a glorious burst of a Hallelujah Chorus, exulting in the praises of the Lamb which was slain from the foundation of the world—yet who is now with his Bride in the glories of the eternal kingdom of God.

Just as the Four Gospels portray the life of the Son of God in the days of his flesh, and just as they point the way for his disciples to walk, so the Epistles, which are addressed to the assemblies of the disciples, exult in the spiritual status of the children of God—and incidentally point out why it is necessary to "put off" some forms of worldly behaviour and to "put on" that which Christ by his Spirit desires to see in the sons and daughters of light. And finally that great drama called the Apocalypse, or Book of Revelation, portrays the victory which the Lamb accomplished on Golgotha and at the empty tomb, the awful efforts of the forces of evil to do away with the witness of the followers of the Lamb, and finally the glorious outcome when all the saints are gathered safely Home in that world which is beyond earthly description.

This is the type of Christian faith and life which Howard Hess Charles seeks to help students to discover on the pages of the Word. This effort the Lord has been pleased to bless in the lives of untold numbers of men and women in Goshen College, in Goshen Biblical Seminary, and in the Associated Mennonite Biblical Seminaries. I count it an honor to be a colleague of this humble teacher of the Word whom our Lord is using so effectively.

To quote Howard Charles himself (1976) as he bares his heart: For many years now I have found in the Scriptures the wellspring of my own faith and life. Poring over their pages I have repeatedly been enlightened, rebuked, exhorted, encouraged, and challenged. Above all I have been pointed beyond the Book itself to him who is the living Word and in whom I have found life. It has been my great joy also to help others listen for his voice through serious and intensive Bible study, and to observe what happens when such dialogue with the Scriptures occurs. It is my constant hope that what goes on in the classroom may be not only an academic exercise but also a meaningful experience of growth in faith and in Christian discipleship.

2

My Spiritual Pilgrimage

Howard H. Charles

In all my years of teaching I do not recall ever being asked to speak publicly in an intimate, personal way about my faith. It has been a meaningful experience to engage in some self-reflection regarding the road I have traveled. I hope also that what I share may be of some help to you.

The topic is somewhat ambiguous. It might be understood to mean either "My Pilgrimage to Faith" or "My Pilgrimage in Faith." Perhaps both ideas were intended. In any case, the topic suggests, and rightly so, that faith and pilgrimage are correlative terms. Faith that is vital is not handed to us ready-made. Search is usually involved. It must be discovered, appropriated, affirmed, or it is not personally meaningful. For most Christians there is a journey, sometimes long, sometimes short, that could be called a pilgrimage to faith.

Life in faith is also a pilgrimage. God has called us to live with him and to share in what he is doing in the world. We do not know in advance in detail what that will mean for us. The journey is through uncharted country. It has an open-ended character. "By faith Abraham," we are told, "went out, not knowing where he was to go" (Heb. 11:8). That is not only the record of one man's experience but also the paradigm of every life lived in genuine faith.

Since this is true, what I will share with you can only be a progress report to date. Twenty years ago, the story would have been somewhat different. Twenty years hence, if the pilgrimage is still in the making, there will doubtless be other differences.

Coming to Faith

Before turning to speak more particularly of my pilgrimage as a

Christian, let me say a word about coming to faith. The journey was not long, agonizing, or dramatic. I had the good fortune of being born into a Christian home in Lancaster County, Pennsylvania. My father, the son of a deacon, was active as a Sunday school teacher in our congregation. My mother, the daughter of a minister, had a healthy interest in the church. Some of my earliest memories cluster around church and Sunday school activities. The Christian instruction of the home and church was supplemented by the contribution of a Christian elementary school teacher. For six of the eight years in a one-room country school I had a Church of the Brethren teacher. She was a good teacher, who felt it important that students memorize Scripture as part of the content of the curriculum. During those years I stored away in memory dozens of verses that have remained with me as a helpful resource.

At the age of nine I felt the call of Christ to become a Christian. After hesitating for some time, I made an affirmative response and was baptized the following year. Though I was quite young, it was a genuine and meaningful experience that did not need to be repeated, as is often the case, at a later period. I remember vividly the exhilaration and joy of those days after having said yes to Christ. My experience was not unlike that of John Bunyan who, after he became a Christian, thought the sun shone more brightly and the birds sang more cheerily than ever before. I, too, was caught up in a world transformed by the living presence and love of Jesus.

Books or the Plow?

After two years of public high school education, my parents offered me the opportunity of completing my high school training at Eastern Mennonite School, Harrisonburg, Virginia. I accepted, and then stayed on for an additional two years of college. Looking back on those four years, I now see them as having been very important in giving shape and direction to my later life. It was then and there that I formed friendships, acquired a deeper appreciation for the church, developed personal convictions, and made basic commitments that continue to sustain and enrich life after these many years.

One experience in particular must be mentioned. During my first year of college, Dean C. K. Lehman called me into his office and suggested that I ought to consider preparing for a church vocation, perhaps teaching. That was a new and an exciting idea. Without making a definite vocational decision, I decided to pursue a college degree. But those plans were changed with the sudden death of my father at the end of the sophomore year. I returned to the farm for the next four years. During that time it gradually became clear that I had more interest in books than in plowing. The farm was sold. I returned to school—this time to Goshen College, Goshen, Indiana.

Call to the Ministry

After graduating from college, I felt an inner urge to go to seminary. In the absence of a Mennonite institution, I chose to go to Union Theological Seminary, Richmond, Virginia. Some years earlier when still a teenager, I had attended an ordination service for a deacon in our district. Suddenly that morning it became clear to me that one day the Lord would call me to be a minister of the gospel.

The usual method for calling ministers at that time in the Lancaster Conference was through the use of the lot. I first participated in this experience during the time when I was on the farm after having finished two years of college. The second time was at the conclusion of the first year in seminary. At the end of the second seminary year, another minister was needed in the district. For the third time I found myself in the class of nominees.

By this time I had become excited about the possibilities of teaching. With two previous escapes, I did not expect to be chosen this time. I was wrong. I was called and ordained to assist the senior minister in the district. He was a man who, although quite elderly, had a liberal spirit and was friendly toward education. When I asked permission to return for the final year of seminary before assuming full pastoral responsibilities, my request was granted. I regarded this permission then, and still do, as a minor miracle.

The Invitation to Teach

The next four years were full of challenge as I settled into the pastoral ministry. To be sure, there were frustations, but basically those were years of growing joy and satisfaction as I sought to serve a responsive congregation in Lititz, Pennsylvania. There were also increasing opportunities for ministry in the larger life of the conference. Probably I would have remained in the pastoral ministry had it not been for the invitation to teach at Goshen College and Seminary, and the interest in teaching that had been kindled in me during my seminary training.

During the last year as pastor at Lititz, I took additional training at Princeton Theological Seminary. This was followed by marriage to a wonderful woman who was then teaching at Goshen College. In the fall of 1947 I settled down to the task that has occupied most of my time and energy until the present time.

It is not my purpose today to give a chronicle of all the varied and interesting things that have happened during the past years. Rather I want to report on some of the significant experiences and important learnings of my spiritual pilgrimage that have come into more or less clear focus for me. There are six observations I should like to share with you.

Indebtedness to Others

First, there has been a deepening awareness of how much of what I am as a Christian person I owe to the contribution of others. Many persons have greatly enriched my life by their friendship, insights, example, and encouragement. While grateful for all, I can mention only a few.

There is my mother who is now in her ninety-eighth year and is still a source of inspiration. She was never in the way when her help was not needed, but never out of the way when it was wanted.

I have had the good fortune of a number of excellent teachers, particularly in college and graduate school. Time will permit reference to only one, the late Professor Howard Tillman Kuist. It was he who, as a teacher in Union Theological Seminary, first kindled in me a genuine excitement for Bible study. He also provided an approach to it that has remained basic in my own study and teaching. Beyond that, he was most helpful on a very personal level during the turbulent experience of the first year when I was being introduced to the critical approach to the Scriptures. My traditional understanding of the Bible was being challenged. Could faith survive? That it did was due in no small measure to the living demonstration of the integration of technical critical scholarship and a vital Christian faith that I saw in Dr. Kuist. If he was able to put the two together, there was hope for me. His example, more than anything else, provided the necessary ballast that kept the ship of faith afloat during that difficult period of reorientation.

My thoughts go back this morning to a small black Baptist congregation in one of the poorer sections of Richmond, Virginia, where I taught a Sunday school class one year while in seminary. The group was small, but warm in spirit. While appreciative of my willingness to share with them, they were aware of my limitations. Each Sunday the session was opened with prayer by one of the officers of the church. I shall not soon forget the prayer offered on one such occasion. With evident sincerity and love, the brother petitioned God on my behalf: "Lord, prop him up on every leanin' side." I believe God not only heard his prayer that afternoon, but has been busy answering it in countless situations ever since.

Another person who comes to mind this morning is Ben Stauffer, a senior member in the Lititz congregation while I was a pastor. I visited him many times as his life gradually ebbed away. Though weak in body he was strong in faith. God was the all-encompassing reality of his daily life. Invariably I came away from his bedroom having received more help than I was able to give.

Again, I remember with much appreciation Mrs. Dugadu, the widow of a former president of the Christian Council of Ghana, with whom I worked on a project in Accra in 1973-74. She was radiant with the Spirit of Christ. Of her I could say, as William James once said of Helen Keller: "The sum of it is, she was a blessing."

Last, but not least in significance, I want to pay tribute to my wife. Let me put it simply: it is hard to imagine what life would have been like these many years without her companionship and love.

Congregational Involvement

The second comment has to do with my relationship to the local congregation where I hold membership. Before coming to Goshen I was deeply involved as a pastor in the life and work of the church which I served. During the first decade as a teacher, the pressure of getting started in the classroom and completing graduate study absorbed nearly all of my time and energy. Consequently, during that period participation in congregational activities was minimal. But in the last two decades there has been a return to a more active involvement in congregational life.

This change has not been accidental. Ever since I became a teacher, I have struggled with the tension between the insistent claims of scholarship on the one hand and the demands of responsible congregational participation and wider church ministry on the other. The Gordian knot might have been cut by invoking the concept of the diversity of gifts and services to excuse myself from the latter involvement. But for various reasons, I could not be happy with that solution.

For one thing, I believe congregational involvement is necessary for personal spiritual health. While it may be possible to stay alive spiritually without meaningful interaction with other Christians, it is certainly not the New Testament ideal. There the individual Christian is always set in the context of the body of Christ. To be Christian is to be committed not only to the Head but also to the members of his body. It is to join with them in corporate worship. It is to be helped toward spiritual maturity through a mutual ministry one to another. It is to be supported in a fellowship of acceptance and love. It is to share with others in a common bond of discipleship and service in which one's own experience and contribution are enriched by association with others. I need congregational involvement to be my best as a Christian.

There is another reason that relates particularly to my work as a Bible teacher. It can be stated in a twofold way. On the one hand, meaningful participation in congregational life is an asset to the process of understanding the Bible. It is not a substitute for the technical tools of academic scholarship, but rather complements them. The Scriptures have come to us out of the community of faith. They speak of what God has done in the past to create a people, and the human response to that action. The inner meaning of this story from the past can be most fully understood as we share experientially in what God is doing now in the continuation of that purpose.

We might, for example, understand Paul's decision to take Titus along to the Jerusalem Conference in this light. The contemporary evidence of God's acceptance of Titus without being circumcised was a helpful clue to the understanding of God's intention in the Old Testament Scriptures. Such a passage as Genesis 17:9-14, where circumcision was the symbol of an everlasting covenant between God and his people, should no longer be pressed to mean that now only men who are circumcised can be included in the people of God. Present-day illustrations of the way experience within the Christian community contributes to the illumination of Scripture might be cited. But I think my point is made.

The other aspect of my relationship as a teacher to the congregation is one of responsibility to serve its needs. The context in which I do my work is not a state university but a church institution. Scholarship is not pursued for its own sake but for the purpose of building up the church. Thus if congregational involvement contributes to my work as a teacher, it is also my hope that as a teacher I can help enrich the life of the larger Christian community in which I participate.

Perception vs. Reality

In the third place, I have learned that perception does not necessarily accord with reality when it is a matter of the how and the where of God building his kingdom. I do not always know on what front God is working or what methods are most effective.

Sometimes God is on the field when he is most invisible. Again, the trumpets may be blowing and the fanfare impressive, but little kingdom work is being done.

This does not mean that we are totally without understanding of the way God proposes to do his work in the world. The Bible surely provides some guidelines and criteria to help us in this matter. But even so our knowledge is often imperfect and our vision dim. Like Elijah at Mount Horeb we expect God to be where the familiar symbols of deity are manifest—strong wind, earthquake, fire—only to discover him when there is no more than a low murmuring sound. Like the two disciples on the way to Emmaus, the Christ of the empty tomb may be our Companion, but we do not have eyes to behold him. Our perceptions do not always faithfully reflect the realities of God's world.

This fact has been underscored repeatedly in my experience. One or two illustrations must be sufficient. Early in my teaching career I taught a course in Romans. One day the session did not go well at all. I felt I was an absolute failure. Back in the office I wondered whether I would ever have enough courage to face that class again. The next day a note was in my mail from a student in the class expressing genuine appreciation for the help received during the period I thought was an utter flop. That experience did not lift responsibility to be the most effective teacher I could possibly be, but it did remind me that there may be discrepancy between my judgment of a situation and what was actually happening.

Some years ago I was asked to speak in a certain congregation. I fulfilled the assignment without indication of any significant results. Only much later did I learn what had actually happened to one person in the pews. He was a former pastor who had left the ministry some years before for another profession. That morning marked the beginning of a turnabout that led him back into the ministry to become an effective pastor. What at the moment seemed routine was not so in retrospect.

I suspect that some day when the full story of our lives is finally unfolded, there will be many surprises. What we now think was crucial may turn out to be not quite so important; conversely, the forgotten or the unknown may then be seen to be quite significant. The point of all this is that we should not take ourselves and our work too seriously. We should, of course, be concerned about faithfulness. But the coming of God's kingdom does not depend wholly on our performance. To believe that God in his own way will achieve his goal, sometimes because of us, and then again in spite of us, is a great liberating experience. I have found it so.

Unanswered Questions

The fourth observation is not totally unrelated to the one just made. It is this: Christian faith can live with unanswered questions. This may sound like a truism since everyone, whether Christian or not, has no choice but to live with mystery. We are surrounded with it all the time. The questions that I have in mind, however, are not in the area of scientific research or what may happen tomorrow, but those related to religious faith—the Bible, theology, ethics.

Most of us have come to seminary seeking answers to certain questions. While in the process of finding some answers we are likely to discover more new questions. Indeed, some earlier affirmations may turn into questions. When Goshen Biblical Seminary was still located on the Goshen College campus, a student on the eve of graduation shared his experience with the seminary community. "During my college days," he said, "I looked with envy at the seminarians with their bulging briefcases. I was sure that they had all the answers safely tucked away in them. Now I, too, have finished seminary. Although I have been able to acquire a briefcase, I still do not have the answers."

He was quite disillusioned. His desire to have answers is understandable. We like security, especially in matters that have to do with our Christian faith. We don't like to say, "I do not know" or, "I am uncertain." Yet in the course of critical inquiry, integrity may demand such a response on more than a few occasions.

Not all questions, of course, are of equal importance. We will save ourselves much frustration if we learn to sort out the really basic or significant questions from the interesting, but more or less unimportant, and then concentrate on the former. I have found much help in a sentence that Bishop J. B. Lightfoot wrote in a letter to a friend in the winter of 1889 just a week before he died: "I find that my faith suffers nothing," said he, "by leaving a thousand questions open so long as I am convinced on two or three main lines." His point was that if one is securely attached at the center, one can afford to sit loosely on the periphery.

Christian faith focuses finally not so much on a set of ideas as on a Person. The heart of what it means to be Christian is best expressed in relational categories. In the prayer language of the Fourth Gospel, ". . . eternal life is this: to know you, the only true God, and Jesus Christ whom you have sent" (17:3, JB). To be firmly anchored in that experiential relationship is not to depreciate in the least vigorous intellectual inquiry. But when again and again the trail of knowledge runs out into the tentative or the unknown, we need not feel threatened.

Discipleship Not Easy

The fifth thing I have learned is that the Christian pilgrimage does not grow easier with the passing of the years. I do not find it easy to live in the company of Jesus. To know that the pattern of discipleship is cut out of the same piece of cloth as Messiahship is a sobering reflection. The road for Jesus led to a cross, and as a disciple of his I am called daily to follow in that way and under that sign. I would not be truthful if I said that obedience to that call comes easy or is automatic. It is not. The temptation is constant to find an easier path. *{Amen}*

There is, for example, the matter of love for God and for my neighbor which, according to Jesus, is God's expectation for me put into a word. I do not know how to meet this demand except to stand daily at the foot of the cross and ask God to renew by his Spirit his love in my heart.

Again, it is clear from the pages of the New Testament and the experience of great Christians throughout church history that prayer is a very important part of vital discipleship. But this, too, I have discovered does not come without effort. It is a discipline that requires constant cultivation.

I must say, also, that Christian hope is not immune to attacks of doubt and cynicism. This is especially true when the eye is focused too steadily on the human scene. There have been times in my experience when Bunyan's description of Christian and Hopeful in the castle of Giant Despair has been meaningful. That story, which has firm New Testament support, has helpful advice for such days.

Alongside this awareness of the high demands of Christian discipleship, which always seem to exceed my grasp, is a complementary growing consciousness and appreciation of the grace of God. Long ago I learned to think of this grace not as an adjunct to my efforts but as the presupposition and framework of my life. I find myself increasingly identifying with a statement made by Professor Hugh Macintosh near the close of his active career as a teacher of theology in New College, Edinburgh. Speaking out of his own deepening experience of divine grace, he said, "I fancy that as we grow older and as we think longer and work harder and learn to sympathize more intelligently the one thing we long to be able to pass on to men is a vast commanding sense of the grace of the

Eternal. Compared with that, all else is but the small dust of the balance."

An Exciting Adventure

The sixth and final word I want to share with you today is that it is a great and exciting thing to be a Christian. It is this precisely because it is a life of pilgrimage. For one thing, it is a pilgrimage into a deeper understanding of the dimensions of the gospel. One is never able to plumb its depths. "How wonderful the gospel of Christ is," said the British preacher R. W. Dale of Birmingham. "I have been thinking about it and preaching about it for more than forty years, and yet there seem to be vast provinces of truth in it which I am only just beginning to explore." That is well said.

Again, to be a Christian is a pilgrimage in becoming one. That may sound paradoxical, but it is true. "A Christian," said B. F. Westcott in his *Commentary on the Gospel of John,* "never 'is' but always 'is becoming' a Christian." To be a Christian is to share not only in something that has happened but in something that is happening and will yet happen. God's purpose is that each of us should bear the likeness of his Son. To that end God was at work in the days of Jesus' earthly ministry and now by his Spirit in each of our lives. This is "process theology" in the biblical sense.

Furthermore, to be a Christian means a pilgrimage in sharing with Christ in what he is doing in the world. I need always to remember that the Christian adventure dare never turn only inward upon my own experience of God's goodness and grace. It must also look outward on the landscape of a world that Christ loved during the days of his flesh and continues to love. You and I are called to be ambassadors of that love in a ministry of reconciliation in a society that desperately needs healing.

In closing let me leave with you some words of Wilbur Webster White, the founder of Biblical Seminary (now New York Theological Seminary), which have provided ongoing stimulus for my pilgrimage. "Abide in Christ and so keep on seeing the invisible, being the unattainable, and doing the impossible." I have never been able to be done with this challenge.

3

The Anomaly of the Prophet

Millard Lind

In the call of Jeremiah, there is an anomaly characteristic of the great prophets in Israel:

"There! I have put my words in your mouth.
See! I have made you an overseer this day
over nations and kingdoms. . ." (Jer. 1:9-10).[1]

In the history of the Near East (indeed in the history of the world) the warrior-king is placed over the nations.[2] How are we to understand that a prophet is placed over the nations, a man whose claim to political power is only that he speaks the word of God?

It is my thesis that this anomaly is to be taken seriously from the standpoint of the theo-political view of ancient Israel. My method is to examine the call of Jeremiah in relation to some other relevant materials of his book. We will then examine the calls of Gideon and of Moses to see if this anomaly can be understood in terms of pre-kingship roots in the history of Israel. This paper only opens up the question, since an adequate treatment demands much more than the allotted space. The relevance of this subject to an understanding of the style of leadership of Jesus and his disciples should be self-evident. It is hoped that the subject is an appropriate one for the event which this book celebrates.

The Call of Jeremiah

The difficulty created by this anomaly is reflected in the history of exegesis. Bernhard Duhm regarded this feature of the call as apocryphal.[3] According to him it was "only the imagination of later Judaism which transformed the modest young priest of Anathoth into the colossal figure who pulls down and builds up nations and kingdoms, and pours out vials of wrath on the whole world."[4] If this is regarded with most modern commentators as authentic to the experience of Jeremiah, is it megalomania?[5] Or does it suggest a new kind of political structure in Israel as compared to the Middle East, a structure in which the prophet rather than the warrior-king is the chief political officer? Is it the prophet's abnormal psychology or is it Israel's unique sociology, specifically her politics, which is responsible for the anomaly?

The causative form of *pāqad* ("make . . . an overseer," J. Bright; "give . . . authority," NEB; "have set . . . over," RSV; "am setting . . . over," JB) occurs approximately twenty-nine times in the Old Testament. Of the twenty-three times the verb is used of people, it is used fifteen times in a "secular" sense of a political or military appointment. Of these occurrences the verb is united with the proposition *'al* (over) comparable to Jeremiah 1:10, in the following passages:

Jeremiah 40:11: had appointed (causative of *pāqad*) Gedaliah. . . . governor over (*'al*—Heb.) them (RSV)

2 Kings 25:22: and over (*'al*) the people . . . he appointed (causative of *pāqad*) Gedaliah . . . governor (RSV)

Genesis 41:34: Let Pharaoh proceed to appoint (causative of *pāqad*) overseers (noun form from the verbal root, *pāqad*) over (*'al*) the land (RSV)

Genesis 39:4: and he made him overseer (causative of *pāqad*) of (over, *'al*—Heb.) his house (RSV)

1 Chronicles 26:32: King David appointed (causative of *pāqad*) him and his brethren . . . to have the oversight of (over, *'al*—Heb.) the Reubenites (RSV)

Joshua 10:18: and set (causative of *pāqad*) men by (over, *'al*—Heb.) it to guard them (RSV)[6]

In light of this usage and of its context in Jeremiah 1:10, the term in this passage can hardly mean other than official appointment, an appointment to an office over the nations. This great prophet in Israel, unique to the Near East so far as we know, was regarded by Israel as Yahweh's chief political officer.[7] As Yahweh's official, he is placed over the nations to destroy and to build.

While the prophet is Yahweh's political officer, set over the nations of the world, we dare not forget the anomaly. The basis of his power is not military force (he has none), but the word of God: "There! I have put my word in your mouth. See! I have made you an overseer this day over nations and kingdoms." It is this anomaly which is strange to the history of the Near East, and indeed of the world. Political power is here ultimately based not on an office representing violent power, but on an office whose only power is the word of God.

Jeremiah recognized that Yahweh also had other political officers. The place of violent political power was seen early in his ministry.[8] Identified first with "all the kings of the North" (Jer. 1:15),[9] this officer was later identified as Nebuchadnezzar of Babylon, the "servant of Yahweh" (Jer. 27:6, *a'bdî*, "my servant").[10]

Three times Jeremiah represents Yahweh as calling Nebuchadnezzar "my servant" (*a'bdî*).[11] One of the most dramatic, and perhaps authentic of these, is his oracle to the council of nations gathered at Jerusalem: "Now I have given all these lands into the hand of Nebuchadnezzar, the king of Babylon, my servant, . . . (*a'bdî*, 27:6, RSV). If Jeremiah had had the usual Near Eastern understanding of the relationship of political power to deity, he need only have heard Yahweh say in his call, "See, I have made Nebuchadnezzar overseer this day over nations and kingdoms. . . ." This avoidance of the anomaly would have made Yahweh's choice of Nebuchadnezzar analogous to Marduk's choice of Cyrus.[12]

In harmony with the anomaly, however, is Jeremiah's dramatic oracle of the destruction of Babylon (51:59ff.), likely given in the very year of his oracle to the nations.[13] The kingdom of Babylon, whose violent political power as wielded by Nebuchadnezzar was Yahweh's servant to subject the nations, would itself be brought to an end by violent political power. It is an illustration of what was later formulated, "He who takes the sword shall perish by the sword." While Jeremiah saw Nebuchadnezzar as an officer of Yahweh, Nebuchadnezzar did not represent the central office in Yahweh's kingdom, and the choice is therefore not parallel to Marduk's election of Cyrus. Jeremiah's positive oracles concerning Nebuchadnezzar are not in conflict with the oracle in regard to his own office.[14]

Another political officer of Yahweh recognized by Jeremiah was King Josiah. Had Jeremiah envisioned with Josiah that the way to the future was via the revival of the Davidic empire, he might have shared the enthusiasm of the Deuteronomic historian for Josiah's reform (2 Kings 23:1-25). The oracle of his call would have fit the spirit of the times at the beginning of Jeremiah's ministry,[15] had he stated, "See! I have made Josiah an overseer this day over nations and kingdoms. . . ."

Since Jeremiah thought well of Josiah (22:15-16) his criticism of Josiah's reform is all the more striking (3:6-10). The messianic theme is shrunken down by Jeremiah (23:5-6, 33:14-18) and the martial character of the future ruler is not his point. It is evident that the king as known to Near Eastern states is not central to his thought of the future.[16]

While the messianic theme is not emphasized by Jeremiah, the positive oracles of the future of Israel and the surrounding nations are in keeping with the prophet's anomalous office. Israel is called to return to Yahweh so that the patriarchal promise might be fulfilled: "Then nations shall bless themselves in him, and in him shall they glory" (4:1-2).[17] The planting of the peoples again in the land is dependent not upon their military prowess but upon their learning the ways of Yahweh's people: ". . . if they will diligently learn the ways of my people, . . . then they shall be built up in the midst of my people" (12:14-17).[18]

One of the greatest of Jeremiah's oracles is the promise of the new covenant (31:31-34).[19] While it deals only with Israel, it sets forth in a striking way the goal of the Old Testament. Contrary to the view of Wellhausen, Jeremiah does not here break out of the confines of a "state religion" to a religion of the heart of the individual.[20] The passage deals not merely with the individual but with God and people. As in the life of any community, law is still necessary. The point is, however, that violent power for the enforcement of law is replaced by voluntary response to the word of God. Law is "written upon the heart." Thus this great passage corresponds to the anomalous character of the prophetic call in chapter 1. In chapter 1 the prophet is placed over the nations, ruling not as a representative of violent power, but by the word of God; in chapter 31 the people respond to law not as enforced by police power, but as a response to an inner reconciliation to that law, with an inner motivation to obey it.

This anomaly of Jeremiah was an accepted reality not by Jeremiah alone, but was acknowledged by Israel's structured institutions. This is evident from Jeremiah's court trial in the accession year of King Jehoiakim (Jer. 26).[21] Saved from a lynching by the princes, Jeremiah was brought by them into court. His defense against the charge that he had "contradicted a cardinal dogma of the official state religion"[22] was not to deny that he had contradicted it, but simply to rest his case on the claim that Yahweh had sent him to speak these words. Jeremiah made this claim both at the beginning and at the end of his defense: "Yahweh sent me to prophesy . . . all the words you have heard" (26:12); "Yahweh sent me to you to speak all these words . . ." (26:15). The princes and "all the people" gave the verdict of "not guilty," a verdict which they based upon this very defense (v. 16).

This anomaly of the prophet was a fact not merely of Jeremiah's time but was a structure which his generation had inherited from the past. This is made clear by the decision of the court, a decision in line with the legal precedent of the prophecy of Micah of the eighth century B.C. (26:17ff.). The statement of this precedent makes clear the place of the prophet in the political structure of Israel. Micah had spoken to all the people of Judah as messenger of their ruler, Yahweh (26:18). The prophet was not put to death by the community. Rather, the representatives of the community's structures feared Yahweh, and brought their policy in line with Yahweh's demand. The prophet addressed himself to all the people in opposition to national policy. This right was acknowledged by both the judiciary (seventh century) and by the king (eighth century), to the extent that, in the latter case, national policy was changed. Consequently, it was not merely the psychology of the prophet which distinguished him from the prophets of the Near East, but more importantly the unique role he played within the structure of Israel's government.[23]

This tie with Israel's ancient past was a strong element in the consciousness of Jeremiah and was clearly stated in his opposition to Hananiah, the self-styled prophet: "The prophets who preceded you and me from ancient times prophesied war, famine, and pestilence against many countries and great kingdoms" (28:8). The close resemblance of his call to the call of Moses suggests that he saw himself in the tradition of Moses.[24] We will now look at that ancient past to see if this anomalous character of the prophetic office is found there.

The Call of Gideon

The call of Gideon forms a common literary pattern with the call of Moses and with the later prophets.[25] The similarity of the form of the call of Gideon to that of Moses suggests the probability of a preliterary (or literary) form of the call in prekingship times.[26] The outstanding difference of this call from the prophetic call has to do not with the form, but with the content. For this call presents no anomaly whatsoever. It is the call of a *môšîᵃ* ("deliverer," cf. Judg. 6:14, 15), a *gibbôr heḥáyil* ("mighty warrior," 6:12). The logical outcome of such a call is kingship, which is precisely what is stated in the subsequent material: "Then the men of Israel said to Gideon, 'Rule over us, you and your son and your grandson also; for you have delivered (*hôšaʿtānu*) us out of the hand of Midian'" (8:22).[27]

Wolfgang Richter proposes that this prophetic call (Judg. 6:11b-17) was adapted to the *môšî*a* and inserted into the segment on Gideon after the time of kingship. The writer was interested in promoting royal authority during the prekingship confederation as derived not directly from Yahweh. Elsewhere this authority is always communicated through the prophet, as indicated by the narrative of Samuel's anointing of Saul (1 Sam. 9-10:16), which follows the same schema as the prophetic call. This suggests that the prophet or seer in the amphictyony had full authority to call a deliverer, who might then be anointed as *nāgîd* (military leader). The prophet was thus important to the institution of warfare for whose execution the *nāgîd* was installed. The latter office developed into kingship, in which the rite of the prophet's calling of the *nāgîd* was replaced by the rite of the enthronement of the king, a development with which the Northern Kingdom did not go along. The later insertion by the writer of a direct prophetic call, instead of a call through a prophet, into the story of a *môšî*a* (according to Richter) was a part of the tendency to make the king independent of prophetic authority.[28]

The advantage of Richter's hypothesis is that it shows the call of Gideon to be a part of the same tendency in early Israel as the Shechemite demand for kingship (8:22).[29] Contrary to Richter, however, there is the probability that the text reflects an historical memory, and was due to the mixing of the Israelite and Canaanite traditions. As in the story of Abimelech (9:1-57), the Gideon pericope evidences a process of the "Israelizing" of the mixed Canaanite population in the tribal territories of Ephraim and Manasseh.[30] That the influence did not go in one direction only is apparent by the fact that Gideon's father had erected an altar to Baal (6:25-32). It is unnecessary to posit with Richter that a later writer from the time of kingship made a literary transfer of the prophetic call from the prophet to the *môšî*a*, for such pressures to "Canaanize" Israel's tradition were already present in the time of Gideon himself.

The relationship of the call of a military deliverer to the office of kingship is evident in the literature of the ancient Near East. In the *Enuma Elish* the father of the gods, Anshar, named Marduk "the hero" as the one who would be able to meet the threat of Tiamat:

He whose [strength] is potent shall be [our] avenger,
He who is *keen* in battle, Marduk, the hero![31]

Called by the gods to meet this threat, Marduk demanded and was given the powers of kingship in order to perform his task.[32]

Hammurabi tells of his call by Anu and Enlil:

... to cause justice to prevail in the land, to destroy the wicked and the evil, that the strong might not oppress the weak, to rise like the sun over the black-headed (people), and to light up the land.[33]

In relation to external powers he was to make "the four quarters of the world subservient. . . ."

A parallel to the predestination of Jeremiah is stated in an ancient Sumerian royal hymn, "King am I; from the womb a hero am I."[34]

In the Egyptian texts there is a stele of King Pianchi (25th dynasty, c. 751-730 B.C.) in which the god Amon speaks to the king:

It was in the belly of your mother that I said concerning you that you were to be ruler of Egypt; it was as seed and while you were in the egg, that I knew you, that (I knew) you were to be Lord.[35]

When there was no question as to the succession, a "call" may not have been necessary; but when a new dynasty was founded (as in the case of Gideon's temptation), or some irregularity occurred, the king's authority needed augmentation by a special manifestation of divine authority. Perhaps because of an irregularity, Thut-Moses III gave at length his call to kingship:

. . . (The god Amon)—he is my father, and I am his son. He commanded to me that I should be upon his throne, while I was (still) a nestling. He begot me from the (very) *middle* of [his] heart [and chose me for the kingship . . . There is no lie], there is no equivocation therein—when my majesty was (only) a puppy, when I was (only a newly) weaned child who was in his temple, before my installation as prophet had taken place. . . .[36]

From these comparisons, it is apparent that the call of Gideon as a *môšiʿa* represented no anomaly whatsoever. The pressures of such ideas pushed into Israel from every side. The anomaly of Gideon was that even as warrior he relied mainly upon the miracle of Yahweh, and that, though called of Yahweh, he rejected the logical eventuation of that call—kingship (8:22ff.). In a negative way, the narratives of Gideon confirm the anomaly of the prophet, that is, that the *môšiʿa* was not to be placed over the nation. The interpretation of a later demand for a change to kingship might be instructive here: "And the Lord said to Samuel, 'Hearken to the voice of the people in all that they say to you; for they have not rejected you, but they have rejected me from being king over them'" (1 Sam. 8:7).[37] By rejecting the seer or prophet and by substituting a king as Yahweh's chief political officer, Israel was rejecting the kingship of Yahweh himself. Later conflict between king and prophet had to do with this issue.[38]

The Call of Moses

The anomaly of the call of Jeremiah is evident in the call of Moses, especially as presented by the J narrative.[39] In the call as set forth by J,[40] Yahweh announces to Moses that he has seen and heard the plight of his people in Egypt[41] and has come down to deliver them from the hand of the Egyptians (3:8). Moses is then commissioned to go, assemble the elders of Israel and to tell them Yahweh's resolve to bring them out of their slavery in Egypt (3:16-17). Moses' first objection, according to J, had to do with his rejection by his people as their political leader (4:1), an objection which Yahweh promised would be overcome by signs (4:2-9). His second objection had to do with his problem of speech (4:10-12) while the third objection was an outright refusal of the task (4:13). Moses did not have the eloquence necessary to accomplish the warrior's task!

It is evident that for J, Yahweh was the deliverer and that Moses was simply Yahweh's messenger to convey his word to his people and, secondarily, to Pharaoh. For J, Yahweh did not deliver his people by means of a warrior, but by a messenger who merely spoke his word.

The E narrative is essentially no different, though Moses is given a more prominent role as deliverer. Yahweh announces to Moses that he has heard the outcry of the people of Israel and has seen the oppression of the Egyptians (3:9). Unlike J, E says that Moses was commissioned to go not to Israel (see 3:16) but to Pharaoh (3:10). Also unlike J who says that Yahweh will bring up his people from Egypt (3:17), E ascribes this function to Moses (3:10). Too much should not be made of this difference, however, as it is evident that for E, as well as for J, Moses was not a warrior, but simply a messenger who spoke Yahweh's word.[42] Yahweh alone performed the warrior's function.

Moses' objection, according to E, had to do with the credibility of his task in regard to Pharaoh: "Who am I that I should go to Pharaoh, and bring the sons of Israel out of Egypt?" (3:11). This is a similar type of objection to the one found in the call of Gideon and of Jeremiah. God's answer to the objection is also similar: "But I will be with you . . ." (3:12). This formula expresses the fundamental structure of Israel's thought and piety.[43] While it does not belong exclusively to the life situation of warfare, this was nevertheless one concretization of the presence of God with one whom he accompanies. A study of the prophet's relation to warfare overlooks

Israel's most unique and fundamental relationship if it overlooks this anomaly of the call of Moses.[44] Armed only with the word of Yahweh, Moses went forth simply as Yahweh's envoy to proclaim freedom both to his people and to Egypt. This act of Israel's history is foundational to Israel's confession of her history: "I am the Lord your God who brought you out of the land of Egypt." Yahweh, not man, is the warrior God who saves his people. The prophet is only the herald of that which God is about to do. This is what both J and E have to say.

Is this prophetic anomaly an event of history? One can only point out that this is Israel's unanimous testimony, including her very oldest testimony. Martin Noth writes, "J formulated the commission to Moses long before the appearance of 'classical' prophecy; thus at this early stage the arrival of a messenger of God who was sent to precede an imminent divine action was not unknown to Israel."[45] Since both J and E are in agreement in regard to this anomaly, one might assume that this was the testimony of G (the foundation document behind J and E), and that this was Israel's tradition before the fall of Shiloh.[46]

The importance of this anomaly of the prophet is evident when one compares Exodus 1-24 with the *Enuma Elish*, both of which have approximately the same value for understanding the structures of their respective societies.[47] Both see divinity as warrior fighting against the enemy. Both emphasize the kingship of the divinity in connection with the victory. Both eventuate in an ordered society. In the Exodus story, however, the action of Yahweh is not against other cosmic powers, but is immediate upon the human scene against the historical enemy of Israel, without the human correspondent of warrior and king. The only herald to Israel and to the foreign power of what Yahweh is about to do is the prophet. Not Yahweh's action in history, but the quality of his act expressed in this new structure is the uniqueness of Israel, both in the ancient and modern world. The figure of the prophet is essential to that uniqueness.

Years ago, Howard Charles pointed out to me that the leadership of Jesus' disciples is to be in contrast to leadership as it was known among the nations: Jesus said, "You know that those who are supposed to rule over the Gentiles (nations) lord it over them, and their great men exercise authority over them. But it shall not be so among you; but whoever would be great among you must be your servant, and whoever would be first among you must be slave of all" (Mk. 10:43-44 cf.; Mt. 20:25-27; Lk. 22:25-27). It is a long journey from Moses to this statement of Jesus, a journey beyond the scope of this paper. That the journey is via the anomaly of the prophet Jeremiah, however, (as representing the anomaly of all the prophets)[48] I have no doubt.

Notes

[1] This translation is that of John Bright, *Jeremiah (Anchor Bible,* New York: Doubleday, 1956), p. 3.

[2] *Enuma Elish;* also the introduction to the law code of Hammurabi. These are discussed below.

[3] Discussed by John Skinner, *Prophecy and Religion: Studies in the Life of Jeremiah* (Cambridge: University Press, 1951), p. 29.

[4] *Ibid.*

[5] Walter Harrelson in *Jeremiah, Prophet to the Nations* (Philadelphia: Judson Press) admits that "this may sound like megalomania . . ." (p. 18).

[6] This usage is not really parallel with the others, as it has to do with a temporary military assignment rather than an appointment to an office.

[7] G. Ernest Wright, "The Nations in Hebrew Prophecy," *Encounter* 26 (1965): 225-237.

[8] Jeremiah 1:13ff., cf. John Bright, *op. cit.,* pp. 7f.

[9] *Ibid.,* p. 6.

[10] For a discussion of this term, see David Noel Freedman, "The Slave of Yahweh," *Western Watch* 10 (1959):1-19.

[11] Jeremiah 25:9; 27:6; 43:10. Could it be that later Jewish resistance to this designation of Nebuchadnezzar is represented by the fact that the LXX avoids it in every case?

[12] *ANET* (1969) p. 315.

[13] For a discussion of these dates, see John Bright, *op. cit.,* pp. 201, 210-212.

[14] For the disharmony of prophet and kingship in Israel see Baltzer, note 38 below. This disharmony is even more pronounced in regard to kingship outside of Israel.

[15] Usually set about 627. Bright, *op. cit.,* p. 84.

[16] *Ibid.,* p. 115.

[17] John Bright regards this as authentic to Jeremiah and places it before 622. See *ibid.,* pp. 25f.

[18] Wilhelm Rudolph regards verses 15-17 as not from Jeremiah, but as a later addition—*Jeremia (HAT),* 3rd ed., p. 90. But see Weiser, *Das Buch des Propheten Jeremia (ATD),* 1960, p. 107.

[19] For comment on its authencity, see Bright, *op. cit.,* p. 287.

[20] Wellhausen, *Prolegomena to the History of Ancient Israel* (Meridian Books, N.Y., 1957), p. 491.

[21] John Bright, *op. cit.,* pp. 167ff.

[22] *Ibid.,* p. 172.

[23] James G. Williams, "The Social Location of Israelite Prophecy," *Journal of the American Academy of Religion* 37 (1969): 153-165.

[24] William Holladay, "The Background of Jeremiah's Self-Understanding, Moses, Samuel, and Psalm 72," *JBL* 83 (1964): 153-164; Rolf Rendtorff, "Erwägungen zur Frügheschichte des Prophetentums in Israel," *Zeitschrift für Theologie und Kirche* 59 (1962): 145-167. Especially N. Habel, "The Form and Significance of the Call Narrative," *ZAW* 77 (1965): 305ff.

[25] Ernst Kutsch, "Gideons Berufung und Altarbau, Jdc. 6, 11-24," *Theologische Literaturzeitung* 81 (1956): 79.

[26] Habel, "Call Narrative," p. 305.

[27] For a review of the history of the exegesis of Judges 6-8, see Wolfgang Richter, *Traditionsgeschichtliche Untersuchungen zum Richterbuch* (Bonn: Peter Hanstein, Verlag GMBH, 1966), pp. 112-114. For Richter's own analysis, see *ibid.,* pp. 114-121. Richter is too negative in his analysis. (See Jacob M. Myers, "The Book of Judges," *IB* 2:678ff., 729, 731.) For a treatment of the tradition in 8:22, 23 see Richter, *op. cit.,* pp. 235f. Such scholars as Martin Buber and H. J. Kraus regard this tradition as a genuine memory. Martin Noth argues that some such prejudice must have existed to keep Israel from accepting kingship for two full centuries after the tribes had settled down, (*The History of Israel,* 1958, p. 165).

[28] Richter, *op. cit.,* pp. 153ff.

[29] We have already suggested such a tie above.

[30] Jacob M. Myers, *op. cit.,* p. 751.

[31] 2:94f. Translation by E. A. Speiser, *ANET* (1969), p. 64.

[32] 2:122-129; 4:1-30, *ANET* (1969), pp. 64, 66.

[33] From the introduction to the code of Hammurabi. See *ANET* (1969), pp. 164-165. We cannot know whether the call came "direct" or through a cultic medium, though the latter possibility is not mentioned.

[34] Samuel N. Kramer, "The Oldest Literary Catalogue," *BASOR* no. 88 (December 1942), p. 14. Cited by Hyatt, "The Book of Jeremiah," *IB* (1956), p. 800.

[35] Translated by M. Gilula, "An Egyptian Parallel to Jeremiah 1:4-5," *VT* 17 (1967): p. 114.

[36] *ANET*, pp. 446f. The word translated "prophet" in the quote, *hem-netjer* "Servant of the god," was a high temple officiant. See *ANET*, Note 1.

[37] This account is usually regarded as a late source. See George B. Caird, "The First and Second Books of Samuel," *IB* 2:917. That it reflects an ancient criticism of the kingship, however, is suggested by I. Mendelsohn, "Samuel's Denunciation of Kingship in the Light of the Akkadian Documents from Ugarit," *BASOR*, no. 143 (October 1956), 17-22.

[38] Klaus Baltzer has suggested that the offices of prophet and priest and king are not so harmonious as often supposed. "Especially the origin, tradition, historical development, and theological implications of the office of the prophet and of the king necessitate competition. It is of fundamental importance to recognize that the concept of the kingship of Yahweh by no means has its presupposition in the earthly Davidic kingdom, but rather is linked with the prophet as his vizier—" "Considerations Regarding the Office and Calling of the Prophet," *Harvard Theological Review* 61 (1968): 581. While prophet as vizier might be debatable, (see James F. Ross, "The Prophet as Yahweh's Messenger," *Israel's Prophetic Heritage,* ed. by Bernhard W. Anderson and Walter Harrelson [1962], pp. 98-107) the rest of the statement is nevertheless correct.

[39] M. Noth sees two sources in this call, as follows: J: 3:1-4a, 5, 7, 8ad, (8abd), 16, 17ad, (17abb), (18-22); 4:1-4, (5), 6, 7, (8, 9), 10-12, (13-16). E: 3:4b, 6, 9-14, (15) . . . ; 4:17, 18 (*A History of Pentateuchal Traditions,* trans. by Bernhard W. Anderson [Englewood Cliffs, N.J., 1972], pp. 30, 36). M. Habel disagrees with Noth, arguing for the unity of 3:1-6, E. Even if one is to accept Noth's analysis, however, E has all the major features of Gideon's call. See M. Habel, "The Form and Significance of the Call Narratives," *ZAW* 77 (1965): 301ff.

[40] Habel's analysis of what he calls the "Yahwist Expansion" is as follows: (1) Introductory Word, 3:7, 8; (2) Commission, 3:16, 17 (18-22); (3) First Objection, 4:1; (4) Signs, 4:2-9; (5) Second Objection, 4:10; (6) Reassurance, 4:11-16; (7) Signs? 4:17 (*Ibid.,* p. 303, note 18).

[41] Noth regards the theophany as also belonging to J. See above, note 39. For a discussion of the theophany, see D. N. Freedman, "The Burning Bush (Exod. 3:2-3)," *Biblica* 50 (1969): 245-246.

[42] While the various sources set forth different details in regard to the escape from Egypt, all agree on the essential point that the escape was due not to an act of war on the part of Israel but on the part of God. For both J and E, Moses was simply an envoy. See Martin Noth, *Exodus* (Philadelphia: Westminster Press, 1962), pp. 40, 41. Also page 119 where Noth speaks of the consensus of the sources in regard to the escape at the sea. See M. Lind, "Paradigm of Holy War in the Old Testament," *Biblical Research* 16 (1971): 16-31.

[43] Horst Dietrich Preuss, ". . . ich will mit dir sein!" *ZAW* 80 (1968): 154.

[44] Von Rad's study of holy war *(Der heilige Krieg im alten Israel)* ignores this most fundamental relationship of the prophet to holy war. He does not deal with this obvious connection because of his presuppositions regarding Israel's early testimony: *Old Testament Theology* 1:107. Quoting Tröltsch sympathetically, he says, "The means by which criticism is at all possible is the application of analogy . . . but the omnicompetence of analogy implies that all historical events are identical in principle."

[45] Martin Noth, *op. cit.*, p. 40.

[46] Noth, *A History of Pentateuchal Traditions*, p. 39: "Everything in which J and E concur can be attributed with some certainty to G."

[47] The question of the original unity of this material is not the point here.

[48] For example, see Hosea 12:13:

By a prophet the Lord brought Israel up from Egypt, and by a prophet he was preserved.

4
The Afterlife of the Ninth Plague (Darkness) in Biblical Literature[1]

J. J. Enz

In the literary and form-critical analyses of the material of Exodus, only spotty attention has been given to the impact of Exodus traditions on subsequent materials in the Bible. Brevard Childs in *The Book of Exodus: A Critical, Theological Commentary* has reminded us of this dimension of the exegetical task.[2]

We propose here an examination of the ways in which the motif of darkness in the ninth plague (Ex. 10:21-29) is developed in later biblical literature. H. P. Müller has shown convincingly that the plagues in the Book of Revelation are dependent on those in Exodus not only as to content but also as to form. They are practically the only occurrences of transmuted magical texts in the biblical canon.[3]

Earlier, G. Kuhn had noted how the Wisdom of Solomon had given to the plagues an apocalyptic and eschatological interpretation. Kuhn demonstrated a close relationship between the use made of the plague material in the pattern of sevens in the Book of Revelation and the reduction of the ten plagues of Exodus to seven in the Wisdom of Solomon.[4] The relationship between Exodus and apocalyptic thinking has been stressed by G. Edwards who noted that "the basic pattern of apocalyptic thought derives from the pattern of the Exodus activity."[5]

The relationship between the plagues and the Gospel of John has been previously examined.[6] By way of comparison with the Book of Wisdom, G. Ziener showed that John's Gospel very probably intended a correspondence between the signs of Exodus and the signs in John. John appears to show an awareness of seven signs in practically the same sequence as does the Wisdom of Solomon.[7]

One is indeed inclined to ask whether the Gospel of John with its presentation of positive signs represents a sharp reaction to the apocalyptic use of the plague motif, as is the case in the Book of Wisdom and in the Book of Revelation.

If so, this would surely be an illustration of the operation of "inner theological criticism" in the Bible as pointed out by B. Childs.[8] Not only is there restricted use of the plague material in the rest of the Bible, as Childs points out,[9] there is also a transformation of the early tradition. This goes beyond Childs to a deliberate inner theological criticism evident in the Gospel of John. In the Fourth Gospel, signs of healing rather than of judgment appear to be operative and they contrast, as well as repeat, the use of the plagues found in the Book of Revelation.

I

To my knowledge previous work has concerned itself mainly with the Exodus signs-plagues as a whole.[10] The task remains to observe the place and function in biblical literature of the individual plagues. Thus this paper addresses itself specifically to the ninth plague—the plague of darkness.

As in the plagues of hail and locusts, the seventh and eighth plagues, the plague of darkness consists of elements from both J and E. The E source shares with the P source, as over against the J source, a formulaic usage involving the jussive (indirect imperative) use of *hāyāh*. The expression *wîhî* ("that there may be darkness," 10:21) occurs also in 9:22 in connection with hail, both instances in E material. P evidences the same formula in 7:9 (rod becoming serpent, reading with the Samaritan text), in 7:19 (water becoming blood), in 8:12 (gnats), and in 9:9 (boils); the latter two render the converted perfect *wĕhāyāh*.[11]

From a form-critical point of view, Müller sees in these expressions the reflection of an earlier folkloristic presentation of the exercise of magic.[12] The only other evidence of this form in the Old Testament is in Genesis 1:3: "And God said, 'Let there be light.'" In both cases the magic formula has been completely absorbed into a Yahwistic confession of faith.[13]

The plague of darkness is located at a climactic point in the series. The response of Pharaoh to this plague is to break off further contact with Moses (10:28f.). This is immediately followed by the tenth plague which is documented (11:1-12:36), by contrast, in much greater length than any of the previous plagues. Attention has been called to the anticipation in the ninth plague of the darkness which shrouded the slaughter of the firstborn in the last plague.[14] On the other hand, the complete silence of the plague of darkness may be contrasted with the outcry at the death of the firstborn.[15] In fact, the last three plagues, of which the ninth plague forms the center, have darkness as an essential part; the swarms of locusts of the eighth plague bring darkness (Ex. 10:15).

II

We turn now to the observation of the impact of the ninth plague on other parts of the Bible. A psalm of thanksgiving and praise, possibly composed in preexilic times,[16] reduces the ten plagues to seven[17] (Ps. 105:28-36). The crucial position of the ninth plague in Exodus, as noted above, may explain the initial position of the plague of darkness in the series in this psalm. Only with the recital of this plague is attention called to Egypt's rebellion:

He sent darkness, and made the land dark;
  they rebelled against his words. (Ps. 105:28)

This reflects the sharp encounter with Pharaoh after the ninth plague (Ex. 10:27ff.). Thus this plague fastened itself in the cultic memory of Israel.

Darkness, as the experience immediately preceding world judgment, has been observed at several points in the prophets.[18] Amos 8:9, in anticipation of the withering judgment recorded in chapter 9, has:

"And on that day," says the Lord GOD,
  "I will make the sun go down at noon,
  and darken the earth in broad daylight."

From the days of Josiah the words of Zephaniah similarly position darkness in close relation to world judgment (Zeph. 1:14f.):

The great day of the LORD is near,
  near and hastening fast; . . .
A day of ruin and devastation,
  a day of darkness and gloom, . . .

Isaiah 13:9ff. also associates darkness with the punishment of the world in an oracle directed to Babylon:

Behold the day of the LORD comes, . . .
to make the earth a desolation
  and to destroy its sinners from it.
For the stars of the heavens and
  their constellations
  will not give their light;
the sun will be dark at its rising
  and the moon will not shed its light.
I will punish the world for its evil, . . .

From the postexilic period, Joel twice makes reference to darkness as coming just before the crushing judgment of the day of the Lord (Joel 3:14f.; cf. 2:31):

... the day of the LORD is near
in the valley of decision.
The sun and the moon are darkened,
and the stars withdraw their shining.

Nahum 1:8 similarly speaks of darkness as penultimate to "the full end" before which the Lord will "pursue his enemies into darkness."

From the time of the Exile, Ezekiel pronounces an oracle of judgment on Egypt that speaks of darkness just before the end (30:18f.):

At Tehaphnehes the day shall be dark,
when I break there the dominion of Egypt,
and her proud might shall come to an end;
she shall be covered by a cloud,
and her daughters shall go into captivity.
Thus I will execute acts of judgment
upon Egypt.
Then they will know that I am the LORD.

Here is not only the pattern of penultimate darkness[19] but also a judgment affecting the young of Egypt (see also 30:17 for Egypt's young men falling by the sword). The pattern set by Exodus is also seen in expressions like "execute acts of judgment"[20] and "they will know that I am the Lord."[21]

Again, in Ezekiel's lament over Egypt, darkness is associated with the end (32:7f.):

When I blot you out, I will cover the heavens,
and make their stars dark;
I will cover the sun with a cloud,
and the moon shall not give its light.
All the bright lights of heaven
will I make dark over you,
and put darkness upon your land,
says the Lord GOD.

The lament concludes with the typical Exodus motif in verse 15: "then they will know that I am the LORD." In this passage, judgment against Egypt expands to become world catastrophe.[22]

Jeremiah similarly announces darkness (expressed as absence of light) but against Jerusalem, not Egypt:

I looked on the earth, and lo, it was waste and void;
and to the heavens, and they had no light (Jer. 4:23).

Words of judgment as applied to Yahweh's own people employ terms used against Egypt. This is to be expected in view of Deuteronomy (28:29f.) where the possibility that the "diseases of Egypt" (the plagues are understood here) will come on Israel herself if she is unfaithful.

It must be noted, however, that the pattern of darkness just before the end is broken in the Bible. The Book of Isaiah twice presents light as following the darkness that engulfs Yahweh's people (8:22-9:2 and 60:1-3). S. Aalen refers the darkness of Isaiah 60:2 to the darkness that covered the Egyptians in the Exodus narrative.[23]

Arise, shine; for your light has come,
    and the glory of the LORD has risen upon you.
For behold, darkness shall cover the earth,
    and thick darkness the peoples;
but the LORD will arise upon you,
    and his glory will be seen upon you.
And nations shall come to your light,
    and kings to the brightness of your rising (Is. 60:1-3).

Here, then, we observe light and salvation as the end rather than judgment and catastrophe. This light focused on the people of the Lord is universally available through the Lord's people.

As noted earlier[24] the Book of Wisdom carries forward the plague narratives of the Book of Exodus giving them an apocalyptic and eschatological dimension. The writer of Wisdom addresses God:

For great are thy judgments and hard to interpret;
    Therefore souls disciplined went astray.
For when lawless men supposed they had
    overpowered a holy nation;
They themselves, prisoners of darkness,
    and bound in the fetters of a long night,
Close kept beneath their roofs,
Lay exiled from the eternal providence
                                (Book of Wisdom 17:1f.).
While over them alone was spread a heavy night,
An image of the darkness that should
    afterward receive them;
But yet heavier than darkness were they
    unto themselves.
                                    (Book of Wisdom 17:21)

The position of the plague of darkness in the sequence of seven plagues (compare the pattern of seven reduced from the ten of Exodus in Psalm 105:28-36) is just before the death of the firstborn and the drowning of the Egyptian army in the sea.[25] This raises the clear possibility that the pattern of sevens in the Book of Revelation is tradition-historically related to this apocalyptic pattern. The pattern of seven as related to world judgment is thus not new in the New Testament.[26]

III

Darkness plays a crucial function in all three of the series of seven (seals, trumpets, and bowls) in the Book of Revelation. The sun becomes black in the opening of the sixth seal (next to the last!) according to Revelation 6:12. A third of the light of sun, moon, and stars is darkened (Rev. 8:12) as the fourth angel blows his trumpet. Special note is taken in 8:13 of the climactic character of the last three trumpets. Thus the fourth trumpet stands in a similar relation to the last three as does the opening of the sixth seal to the final seal. The kingdom of the beast is plunged into darkness at the fifth angel's bowl as noted in Revelation 16:10. The position of the pouring of the fifth bowl is again a preparation for the climax in the much more elaborated sixth and seventh bowls. As in the preparatory ninth plague of Exodus where Pharaoh expresses absolute resistance (Ex. 10:27), so here men "cursed the GOD of heaven . . . and did not repent" (Rev. 16:11).

If similarity of form and content is crucial for detecting typological relationship,[27] then the connection between the plagues of Egypt and the judgments in the Apocalypse of John is particularly telling. As we noted above, only in these two series of judgments, the one through the agency of Moses under Yahweh and the other through the agency of angels, is use made of a quasi-magical formula (Hebrew *wayhî*=Greek *Kai egeneto,* lit., "and there was").[28]

The pattern of judgment found in Exodus and the Book of Wisdom persists in the Book of Revelation. The Gospels, however, appear to see the darkness as preparatory for a burst of light, as in Isaiah 60:1-3.

Mark 13:24ff. has:

> But in those days, after that tribulation, the sun will be darkened, and the moon will not give its light, and the stars will be falling from heaven, and the powers in the heavens will be shaken. And then they will see the Son of man coming in clouds with great power and glory.

The position of darkness as just before the climax is maintained; but the final judgment is seen as positive. The parallel passage in

Matthew (24:29f.) is similar. Luke (21:25) without using the term *darkness* speaks of "signs in sun and moon and stars." The term *signs* has its own way of connecting with the Exodus tradition where it is a key word, and used twice to introduce the last three plagues (Ex. 10:1f.) of which darkness is the second. Furthermore, H. Frey[29] has called attention to a similar sequence of darkness immediately preceding the climax (of resurrection) in Luke 23:44f.:

> It was now about the sixth hour, and there was darkness over the whole land until the ninth hour, while the sun's light failed; and the curtain of the temple was torn in two.

Resurrection becomes world salvation as well as world judgment.

Clearly in line with this salvific use of signs in the synoptic Gospels is the Johannine counterpart to the raising of Lazarus, the positive counterpart to the destruction of the firstborn of the Egyptians. Thus light or sight in God's work through Jesus becomes the earnest of life from death. This is the larger canonical criticism of darkness as preparation for death as seen in Yahweh's work through Moses.[30]

This is not to say, however, that the judgmental aspect has been left behind. Smith[31] rightly points to John 9:39, "For judgment I came into this world, that those who do not see may see, and that those who see may become blind." Immediately associated with the sign of giving sight is the negative side—namely, the deepening darkness of unbelief even among the chosen people. This is reemphasized in the final appeal of Jesus to the unbelieving Jews to leave the hardness of heart(!) of their walk in darkness to "believe in the light, that you may become sons of light" (John 12:36). One more reference to darkness comes just before the end, as suggested in the following paragraph:

> When Jesus had said this, he departed and hid himself from them. Though he had done so many signs before them, yet they did not believe in him (John 12:36b, 37).

The unbelieving establishment has become equated with hardening Pharaoh. The believers are the people of God—the "sons of light" in conflict with unbelievers in darkness.[32] Here, then, may also be seen the setting for the eschatological conflict portrayed in the Qumran community's *Rule of War between the Sons of Light and the Sons of Darkness*. Like John, the faithful community is set over against the unfaithful establishment. There is a restricted usage of "sons of light." The expression "sons of darkness" is not found in John or the New Testament as a whole. John is countering a legalistic, ritual-oriented warfare as represented at Qumran with a living, dynamic participation in Yahweh's encounter with evil through Jesus.

In Summary:

1. This presentation calls for attention to a dimension of exegesis called "theological criticism,"[33] or perhaps "dialogical exegesis."

2. The need for such exegesis is expressed through a study of the motif of darkness as that motif comes dramatically to the fore in the ninth plague of the Book of Exodus.

3. It has been noted that the ten plagues of Egypt in the Book of Exodus provide a larger pattern for the seven plagues of Psalm 105, and of the Book of Wisdom, and for the seven seals of the Book of Revelation.

4. The position of the plague of darkness as next-to-the-last is reflected at several points in the prophets: preexilic, exilic, and postexilic. Ezekiel especially stresses Exodus motifs related to the plagues as well as relating darkness to the end.

5. The pattern of darkness followed by judgment as above is broken in Isaiah where light and salvation appear after darkness; this is also the case in the Gospels.

6. The pattern of sevens in judgments is not unique to New Testament apocalyptic in the Book of Revelation. It can be traced to Psalm 105 and to the Book of Wisdom.

7. Especially in the seven seals of the Book of Revelation, darkness is associated with the penultimate seal. In the series of trumpets and bowls, darkness comes before the climactic judgment. Furthermore, only Exodus and the Book of Revelation make use of the same quasi-magical formula, "and there was."

8. The Gospel of John with its series of seven signs in the same order as in the Book of Wisdom also bears a relationship to the plagues of Egypt. The fact that the signs are positive strongly raises the question whether the Gospel of John represents a sharp reaction to the apocalyptic use of the plague motif as well as the use in the Book of Exodus. Thus later use of the plague motif may contrast as well as repeat.

Notes

[1] For the wording of this title and encouragement to prepare this paper I am indebted to correspondence with Waldemar Janzen, Canadian Mennonite Bible College, Winnipeg.

[2] Philadelphia: Westminster Press, 1974. For a monograph devoted to this effort see D. Daube, *The Exodus Pattern in the Bible*. (Salem, N.H.: Faber and Faber, 1963.) Daube selects several narratives from Exodus to observe their use in the rest of the Old Testament.

[3] H. P. Müller, "Die Plagen der Apokalypse," *ZNW* 51 (1960): 268-78.

⁴ G. Kuhn, "Beiträge zur Erklärung des Buches der Weisheit," *ZNW* 28 (1929): 334f. cf. H. Conzelmann, "SKOTOS," in *Theological Dictionary of the New Testament*, vol. 7 (Grand Rapids: Eerdmans, 1971), p. 431.
⁵ G. Edwards, "The Exodus and Apocalyptic," in *A Stubborn Faith: Papers for Andrew Irwin* (Dallas: Southern Methodist University Press, 1956), p. 31.
⁶ Cf. my article, "The Book of Exodus as a Literary Type for the Gospel of John," *JBL* 76 (1957): 210.
⁷ G. Ziener, "Weisheitsbuch und Johannesevangelium (I)," *Biblica* 38 (1957): 415.
⁸ *Op. cit.*, pp. 169f.
⁹ *Ibid.*, p. 162.
¹⁰ Cf. e.g., *Ibid*, pp. 151-164. Brief treatments of the comparisons of individual signs of Exodus with those of the Gospel of John are noted by R. H. Smith, "Exodus Typology in the Fourth Gospel," *JBL* 81 (1962): 334-338; note especially the comparative tabulation of series of signs in Exodus and John, p. 338. (Cp. J. M. Ford, *Revelation*, Garden City: Doubleday, 1975, pp. 265-275.)
¹¹ For a convenient tabulation of these forms see Müller, *op. cit.*, pp. 273ff.
¹² Müller, *op. cit.*, pp. 276f.
¹³ *Ibid.*, p. 277.
¹⁴ Childs, *op. cit.*, p. 160.
¹⁵ *Ibid.*
¹⁶ Cf. M. Dahood, *Psalms III* (Garden City: Doubleday, 1970), p. 51.
¹⁷ Thus the pattern of sevens traced by Ziener (see above) from the Gospel of John to Wisdom is shown to have deeper roots in the O.T.
¹⁸ H. Frey *Das Buch der Heimsuchung und des Auszugs* (BAT) (Stuttgart: Calwer Verlag, 1949), p. 123.
¹⁹ W. Eichrodt comments concerning this passage: "... the darkening of the sky, which covers the city like a cloud, will give the cosmic sign of the end of Egypt, thus repeating the second to the last of the plagues brought upon Egypt by Moses (Ex. 10:21), which will inevitably be followed by God's final blow," *Ezekiel: A Commentary* (Philadelphia: Westminster, 1970), p. 418f.
²⁰ Literally, "to do acts of judgment" (found nine times in Ezekiel) is precisely the expression found in Exodus 12:12 where Yahweh is also the subject of the action in connection with the death of the firstborn in Egypt. In a recital that includes reference to this same event, Numbers 33:4 has the same expression.
²¹ The expression "They (the Egyptians) will know that I am the Lord" occurs at the beginning (Exod. 7:5) and end (Exod. 14:4, 18) of the plague narrative in Exodus; for other expressions of the same motif see Exodus 7:17; 8:22.
²² Eichrodt, *op. cit.*, p. 433.
²³ *Die Begriffe 'Licht' und 'Finsternis' im Alten Testament, im Spätjudentum und im Rabbinismus* (Oslo: Dybwad, 1951), p. 77.
²⁴ See above page
²⁵ G. Kuhn, *op. cit.*, pp. 335ff.
²⁶ *Ibid.*, pp. 334f.
²⁷ Cf. R. H. Smith, *op. cit.*, p. 331. George B. Caird has indeed argued that the sole reason the frogs are introduced into the plagues mentioned in the Book of Revelation is to maintain the sequence of the Egyptian plagues: See *A Commentary on the Revelation of St. John the Divine*, (New York: Harper and Row, 1966), p. 206.
²⁸ Müller, *op. cit.*
²⁹ *Ibid.*
³⁰ Smith states, "The ninth sign which Moses performs is that of invoking darkness upon Egypt (Exod. 10:21-29). With its specific statement that the darkness was so deep that the people behaved as though blind, the Exodus account offers a solid type for the Johannine account of the healing of the blind man (John 9:1-41),

in which Jesus brings sight to one who sits in darkness," *op. cit.,* pp. 336f.

[31] *Ibid.,* p. 337, note 18.

[32] G. Ziener has observed that both John and Wisdom shared a Palestinian Jewish format of the Exodus happenings. In Wisdom, the Egyptians and the Israelites are to be understood typically as the godless and the righteous. In John, the conflict between Jesus and the Jews is representative of the war between light and darkness always transpiring in mankind (*op. cit.* pp. 415-418).

[33] Cf. B. Childs, *The Book of Exodus,* pp. 169 ff.

5

Three Ancient Jewish Attitudes Towards Poverty[1]

J. Massyngberde Ford

In this essay I shall endeavor to examine three attitudes towards poverty in the ancient world. I have chosen as my primary texts (a) Sirach, (b) the Qumran documents, and (c) Mishnaic and Talmudic material.

I. Sirach

Hebrew and Greek Sirach brings one into the world of Ptolemy VII (145-116 B.C.). Palestine was under the Ptolemies from 312-198 B.C. and under the Seleucids from 198-164 B.C. It was a time when Palestine was important not only as a buffer state between the Great Hellenistic powers, but also as a commercial route, the caravan route from Mesopotamia, the Persian Gulf, and Southern Arabia.[2] The forests of Palestine were important for the naval power of the Ptolemies. The land itself had many rich resources. Sirach presents the ideal of life for the Hellenistic Jew, namely, to be rich and at peace.[3]

The book maintains a *via media* between self-aggrandizement through commerce and business and the indignity of poverty. In preexilic Israel and during part of her postexilic period there was a deep-rooted social tradition as a result of the preaching of the prophets which presented a complete contrast to the Greek ideal. "The poor" were frequently identified with the "unjustly oppressed" to such an extent that the word came to mean "righteous," a development which would have been impossible for the Greeks, who recognized responsibility for the family and the *polis* but not for their poverty-stricken neighbor.[4] Bolkestein, who has pursued a careful and comprehensive study on this, finds that unique to Israel were the *gerim,* the aliens living and working in an Israelite

39

community towards whom the Jews felt an obligation.[5] Indeed, only the Israelite names the giving of alms to the poor as one of the virtues.[6] The prophets are passionate pleaders for the poor and they censure usurers as well as the rich farmers, who appropriate all the land, sometimes profiting by unjust verdicts of the judges.[7] On the other hand, Bolkestein finds an affinity between the ideals of Israel which were essentially the same as those in Egypt in contrast to those of Greece.[8] Job mentions almost exactly the same categories as the Egyptians: those in misery, the orphan, the lost, the widow, the blind and lame, and the poor (Job 28:12-17).[9]

With and after the conquest of the East by Alexander, the army had a direct effect upon the economies of the Hellenistic countries. Alexander shared his hoards of Persian gold and silver—often minted into money—with the soldiers who served him. Hence many hitherto "proletarians" gained financially. Soldiers who survived battle looked forward to a life of wealth and prosperity.[10] However, even the moving army was a source of commerce. Many merchants bought booty from the soldiers, and "money flowed freely from the belts of the soldiers into the chests of the civilians and vice versa." Thousands of civilians traveled with the army: wives, concubines, children, servants, slaves, merchants, and money-lenders. The Hellenistic army was "an enormous moving city, comparable to the moving cities of the Oriental nomads in eastern Europe and in Asia."[11] Army officers were mainly very rich and Alexander founded wealthy urban settlements and left many of his soldiers as colonists. These formed a new class of men. Some became tyrants. They were ambitious and invested money in their cities. This military factor is important for Palestine, for in the two decades after the death of Alexander, she was crossed or occupied seven or eight times by armies.[12]

Egypt concentrated her power into the hands of the king, thus forming a state capitalism without parallel in the ancient world. Palestine, too, became the personal possession of the king and the leading places were in the hands of Hellenists. In 2 Maccabees 3:4ff. one finds a dispute between the protector (*prostatēs*) of the temple and the high priest Onias III. This *prostatēs* seems to be independent of the high priest. One meets the *gerousia* for the first time in a decree of Antiochus III. Sirach gives indication of the existence of this body (Sir. 33 [G 30] 27, cf. Josephus, *Ant.* 12:142 cf. 138). It comprised the principal priests, the rich lay nobility, the great landowners and heads of clans, and one may assume that the Tobiads played an energetic part until the outbreak of the

Maccabean revolt.[13] Further, the "court stories," e.g. Nehemiah and Daniel, show an openness to the world on the part of Jews who sided with the secular powers and opposed the nationalists. These Jews are attacked in Sirach 6:17; 9:16; 11:9; 12:14. The social rift between the lower classes and the aristocracy who associated with the foreign powers was severe. This contrast is lamented by the prophets and above all in Koheleth (5:9-6:9). Koheleth comments on the restless businessman who has no time to enjoy his wealth.[14] Nevertheless in the later portion of Proverbs and Ben Sirach, poverty is to be condemned, as in Greece; it is seen as something which people bring upon themselves.

The Jerusalem priesthood itself became a business to some extent; the sons of the high priest became treasurers. This was enhanced by pilgrimages from the diaspora to Jerusalem which created a whole class of bankers and moneychangers for the pilgrim.[15] In addition, the half shekel paid by every male Jew over twenty could have contributed vastly to the wealth of the temple, for Jerusalem was a Temple State. Crassus is reputed to have taken away eighteen million talents worth in gold.[16] Josephus remarks: "No one need wonder that there was so much wealth in our temple for all the Jews throughout the habitable world, and those who worshiped God, even those from Asia and Europe, had been contributing for a very long time" (*Ant.* 14:110; 16:167). Philo intimates that the leading citizens vied with each other for the honor of taking contributions to Jerusalem (*De Spec. Leg.* 1, 14, 78).[17] On the other hand the *Letter of Aristeas* bears witness to the grandeur of the temple although it says that the city was of moderate size. However, one need not see the riches of the temple (to which the Qumran covenanters were so opposed) as unique. Delos and other Greek temples were equally rich, developed their treasuries into a bank, lent money at interest and had lands and houses at their disposal.[18]

This brief sketch should assist us to understand the teaching of Sirach more clearly. Sirach sees moderate wealth as an asset and a blessing to be enjoyed here and now rather than left as an inheritance (10:27, 30; 13:23; 14:11-17; 29:21-22; 40:17). His advice to the president of dinner parties (31:12-31; 32:1-13) may perhaps be understood in the light of such banquets as described by Aristeas. One such banquet lasted seven days and was the occasion of learned conversation. Ben Sirach advises prudence and care for one's material possessions—protection of cattle (7:22); security of property and gold and silver (28:25). He is not in favor of giving property to anyone else (33:20-24). He counsels the keeping of strict accounts over scales and weights, making large and small profits, gaining from business transactions, using one's seal against an interfering wife, locking up possessions, issuing stores by number and weight, and keeping written accounts of spending and taking (42:1-7). One can see this as a vivid contrast to the teaching of Jesus, especially the Sermon on the Mount and the Sermon on the Plain. Yet Sirach issues clear warnings against temptations and misfortunes attending wealth. One must not give one's heart to wealth, regard oneself as self-sufficient (5:1-2; 11:23-27; and 18:25), nor be proud of one's clothing or accomplishments (11:4). It is risky to undertake too much business (11:10-11). Sirach is fully alive to the dishonesty which so frequently accompanied commerce and also to arrogance, exploitation, extortion, deception and being put to ridicule by the rich man (13:3-8, cf. 21-29). He knows the folly and danger of using credit and writes graphically:

To build your house on other people's money is like collecting stones for your tomb (21:8).

Sirach believes that it is difficult for the merchant and salesman to avoid wrongdoing; if necessary they are ruthless:

A peg will stick in the joint between two stones, and sin will wedge itself between selling and buying (27:2).

He also warns about the danger of going surety for one's neighbor (29:14-26). Riches make a person lose weight and sleep, they bring many to ruin:

Happy the rich man who is found blameless . . . since he has achieved wonders among his kind?

Who has been through this test and emerged perfect? . . . Who has had power to sin and has not sinned? . . . (31:8-10).

Sirach gives considerable space to almsgiving and the help of the needy. Many of his maxims appear in the other deuterocanonical literature and later in Mishnah and Talmud where they are elaborated (*vide infra*). Sirach's concern for the poor may be gauged not only by the rift between the classes but also by the harm perpetrated by tax farmers. Collection of taxes was strict; fraud and refusal to pay met with harsh reprisals; informers were generously rewarded; and those who owed taxes were threatened with prison or slavery (Ps. *Arist.* 26). As Baron observes, a few examples of rich Jews and Jewesses must not blind one to the appalling poverty which prevailed among the masses, "the oppressive burden of taxation which made possible all this splendour brought the people of Palestine to the brink of ruin."[19] Each village seems to have been leased to farmers of revenue. Higher in rank than the village chiefs, they were akin to village scribes. They appear to have been in general charge of the revenues of the king, and may also have acted as stewards of the king and been charged with the duty of making contracts for the cultivation of the royal land. Josephus speaks of tax farmers in Syria who were responsible for one or more cities. There seems to have been one man over the whole province as well. [20]

Although Sirach urges help for the poor and destitute it is remarkable that he does not refer to any of the biblical laws of tithing, the forgotten sheaf, the corner, the second gathering, the sabbatical, or the Jubilee year. Sirach sees almsgiving as atonement for sin (3:30). One must give without delay to the destitute, the beggar, and to the poor man (4:1-5 and cf. 7:10). One must deliver the oppressed from the oppressor and greet a poor man courteously (4:8). The poor, both living and dead, must be helped (presumably the dead by burial 7:32-40). Helping the poor will bring reward from God (4:10; 11:22; and 29:8-17). The Lord himself looks after the poor (11:12-23). Loans may be regarded as an act of mercy but creditors may behave in an unseemly manner when their debts are due (29:1-10).

However, merely giving to the poor is not sufficient; one must inculcate the right attitude. One must accompany the present with a kindly word (18:15-18):

Does not dew relieve the heart?
In the same way a word is
worth more than a gift (v. 16).

Charity may even bring earthly benefits, for a poor neighbor will stand by one in adversity and may share a legacy with you (22:23). On the other hand refusal of charity or withholding wages is equivalent to murder (34:21-26). Offering sacrifice from property of the poor "is as bad as slaughtering a son before his father's eyes." However, one is to help neither the sinner nor the godless; one must refuse him bread, for it might make him stronger than oneself and one would be repaid evil twice over: God repays the wicked with vengeance (12:3-7).

Sirach values sure friendship beyond price (6:14) and recognizes the gulf between rich and poor.

Every creature mixes with its kind . . .
What peace can there be between hyaena and dog?
And what peace between rich and poor (13:15-17).
Wild donkeys are the prey of desert lions;
So, too, the poor are the quarry of the rich (13:18).

Finally, Sirach warns against informers for the king or the rich,

presumably tax farmers or dishonest merchants:
> Do not curse the king, even in thought;
> do not curse the rich, even in your bedroom,
> for a bird of the air will carry the news;
> indiscretion sprouts wings.

Thus Sirach stands in contrast to the prophets with their denunciation of social injustice and also in distinction from the covenanters of Qumran who withdrew from the city where the princes of Judah and the priests had grown rich on ungodly gain. Sirach mingles with the world and enjoys it with prudence and wisdom. He is not oblivious to the poor, but neither is he a social activist on their behalf.

II. Qumran

There are three short observations to be made about Qumran and "poverty." First, either 1 QS and CD cater to two different sections of the community or 1 QS is a later and stricter development. Second, "poverty" in the sense of evangelical poverty and the "poverello" does not seem to exist for the Qumran covenant. The covenanters appear to have lived a simple life but with some affluence as seen, for instance, by their possession of writing material, the scrollery, the materials from which their weapons are made—if QM is not an allegory (cf. the shields of bronze adorned with gold, silver, and precious stones 1 QM 5:4-6;[21] the spears of the same material with "pure gold at the centre of the point" 1 QM 5:7; "the swords of purified iron, adorned with pure gold, the hilt of horn the work of an artist [adorned with] a many coloured design in gold, silver and precious stones" 1 QM 5:11-14, and the six thousand stallions 1 QM 6:11). Third, their motive for communal property is to prevent ritual defilement from the less observant Jew or the Gentile: it has little intrinsic value. If the list of treasure on the copper scroll is genuine, the community was certainly affluent.

In CD there is no mention of "mingling property." However, the members are to keep themselves from the "unclean riches of iniquity" which have been gathered from robbing the sanctuary, the poor of the people, the widows, and the orphans (CD 6:15-17, cf. 8:5, and 19 [1] 9-10). They are not to shed the blood of Gentiles for riches or gain unless it is by order of the Council of the Association of Israel. Neither are they to sell clean beasts or birds to the Gentiles in case they should sacrifice them (CD 12:6-11). They are also to refuse the Gentile the contents of the member's granary or vat, or any other goods or slaves or maidservants (*ibid.*). There seems to be an assumption of private property owned and controlled by the members of the sect. Further the members are forbidden to have any dealings with the sons of the Pit (presumably nonorthodox Jews) except by paying from hand to hand, that is to say, there must not be association or contract (CD 13:14-16). However, this buying and selling might be permitted by the overseer (*ibid.*). The members of the community for which CD was written are to support their brothers, the needy, the poor, and the stranger (CD 6:20). There are special funds for charity and the following may avail themselves of them: orphans, the poor, the needy, the old, the fugitive, the captive, the virgin without kin, and the young woman whom no man seeks in marriage. There are no such listings in 1 QS. Each member, however, pays two days wage per month into the charity fund; this, again, presupposes private property and individual work. The funds do not seem to be restricted to the members of the community. However, there is to be no association with the excommunicate, either through property or work (CD 20 [2] 7). Rules for the Sabbath are stricter than in Rabbinic Judaism; one may not lend anything on the Sabbath, nor discuss riches or gain or profane the Sabbath "for matters of riches and gain" (CD 10:18).

1 QS appears to be more exclusive than CD. Everyone, even the novices, are required to separate themselves from perverse men, so that the holy do not rely on the work of vanity (1 QS 5:14-20 cf. 9:7-9 [condemnation of the wicked's hoarding]), and all property comes under the jurisdiction of the sons of Zadok, the priests, and the majority (1 QS 5:2). The property of the novice is shared only at the end of the first year and is completely surrendered only at the end of the second year, when the idea of "mingling of property," a technical term (cf. Josephus, *War* 2:122) comes into play (1 QS 6:22). At the end of the first year the candidate's property is handed over to the overseer of the revenues of the Many. It is inscribed to his credit but is not spent for the profit of the Many (1 QS 6:19). Lying about property is punished by a year's separation and rationing of food (1 QS 6:24), and negligence with regard to the property of the community must be remedied by reimbursement or punishment for sixty days (1 QS 6:6). An excommunicate has no share in the community and none of the men of holiness shall mingle with his possessions or counsels (1 QS 8:22).

Thus I concur with Keck[22] and others that the Qumran community is poor or meek in spirit rather than economically poor.

III. Rabbinic Literature

Rabbinic sources show that, in contrast to Qumran or the New Testament, poverty or communality of goods were by no means an ascetic ideal and desirable *per se*. R. Phinehas b. Hana expounded a text from Job and concluded that poverty was worse than all of Job's fifty plagues (*B.B.* 116a). Mar'Ukba gave away half of his wealth when he was about to die and was commended for this, but the common opinion was that one should not give away more than one-fifth of one's wealth during one's lifetime in order to avoid poverty (*Ket.* 67b cf. 50a). R. Ammi and R. Assi both said that when a man needs support from his fellow-beings, it is as if he were punished with two opposite punishments, with fire and with water (*Ber.* 6b). R. Eleazar ha-Kappar advised praying to be spared the fate of poverty for if it did not descend on a man, either his son or his grandson would suffer the fate. They saw poverty as "a wheel that revolves in the world," (*Shabb.* 151b). R. Nathan b. Abba further said in the name of Rab: "He who is dependent on another's table, the world is dark for him." The Rabbis taught that there were three whose life is no life and these were: "he who is dependent on the table of his neighbor; he whom his wife rules; and he whose body is subject to suffering. And some say: Also he who possesses only one shirt (because he will have vermin)" (*Bez.* 32b). Hence it is undertandable that Rabbinic texts include the poor person among the "dead" (*Ned.* 64b; *A.Z.* 5a, cf. *Erub.* 41b). They consider riches to become the righteous (*Ab.* 6:8) and advise a person to engage much in business and deal honestly (*Nidd.* 706) as well as giving tithes; then he will become rich (cf. the grief that comes with poverty [Ber. 5a] and poverty as a sign of conceit [*Shabb.* 33a]). It was also believed that demons were associated with poverty (*Pes.* 111b; *Hull.* 105b), and that if the sages or the rabbis direct their eyes against one, the consequence would be either death or poverty (M.K. 17b; *Hag.* 5b). It was further taught on the basis of the text "Save that there shall be no poor among thee" that priority is given to one's own lost articles even over those of one's father. That is one must avoid any action that may lead to poverty. The *Shekinah* rests with those who are wise, strong, wealthy, and tall (*Shabb.* 92).

The only type of poverty which appears to have been acceptable is that which was embraced for the sake of scholarship. But even under these circumstances it is believed that there will be a reversal of fortune; those who study Torah in poverty will become rich. (*Erub.* 21b; *Ned.* 49b-50a; *Sanh.* 20a refer to the great poverty of those scholars who lived during the Hadrianic persecution; *Sot.* 49a; *Hor.* 10a; *Ab.* 6:4). Thus:

> Whoever fulfills the Torah out of [a state of] poverty, his end [will be] to fulfil it out of [a state] of wealth; and whoever discards the Torah out of [a state of] wealth, his end [will be] to discard it out of [a state of] poverty (*Ab* 4:8-9 cf. *Yoma* 35b).

It was also taught that one should sell all he has to marry the daughter of a scholar, or the head of a synagogue, or the daughter of a charity treasurer, or an elementary teacher; one should not marry the daughter of an *'am ha'aretz* (*Pes.* 49b).

From this attitude toward poverty arise two important factors: (a) the emphasis on charity or almsgiving (often identified with "righteousness," cf. *Sanh.* 6b) and (b) the acute concern for preserving the dignity of the poor person. Lack of charity was seen as equivalent to idolatry (*Ket.* 68a; *B.B.* 10a). Even the poorest of Israel was not exempt from this duty (*Hull* 131a, cf. *Gitt* 7a). R. Assi said that "Charity is equivalent to all the other religious precepts combined" (*B.B.* 9a). Rewards either in this world or the next were expected for the person who practiced charity, for example, Benjamin the Righteous was purported to have been cured from a serious illness and to have twenty-two more years added to his life because he helped a widow and her seven children (*B.B.* 11a). A man's crops were saved from hail because he gave a *denar* to a poor man on the eve of New Year (*Ber.* 18b). R. Akiba's daughter was saved from a deadly serpent bite because she gave a portion of the wedding feast to a poor man (*Shabb.* 156b). A man gave a coin for charity so that his son might live (*Pes.* 8a cf. *R.H.* 4a). Eclipses were attributed to forgeries, ravaging another's property, and cutting down good trees. Four things were said to cause property to fall into the hands of the government: retaining possession of bills which have been paid, lending money on usury, refusing to protest against wrongdoing when one had the power to do so, and publicly declaring the intention to give specified sums for charity and not carrying it out (*Sukk.* 29a-29b). While one need not give credence to all these reported miracles, they do illustrate the Jewish attitude to the importance of charity.

> R. Eleazar said: When the Temple stood, a man used to bring his shekel and so make atonement. Now that the Temple no longer stands, if they give for charity, well and good, and if not, the heathens will come and take from them forcibly (*B.B.* 9a cf. 10a).

R. Eleazar, son of R. Jose, spoke about charity and deeds of loving-kindness promoting understanding with God the Father and bringing redemption nearer (*B.B.* 102). One may compare *Ber.* 8a: If a man occupies himself with the study of the Torah and with works of charity and prays with the congregation, I account it to him as if he had redeemed Me and My children from among the nations of the world (*Ber.* 8a).

R. Isaac said, "Four things cancel the doom of man, namely, charity, supplication, change of name, and change of conduct" (*R.H.* 16b). It was also believed that one received expiation from sin and a longer life if one engaged in charity (*R.H.* 18a, cf. *Ber.* 5a). On the other hand it was believed that one suffered punishment if one did not perform charity, or did so for the wrong reason (*Ket.* 66b-67a, cf. *B.B.* 10a). It was taught that one who dispenses charity is delivered from Gehenna: he is like a shorn sheep who finds it easier to cross a river than one who is not shorn (*Gitt.* 7a). King Monobaz of Adiabene distributed his father's inheritance in a time of scarcity and to his brother's complaints he replied that he stored treasure above where it could not be tampered with and that he gathered a harvest of souls, that he stored up for the future world (*B.B.* 11a, cf. *Sanh.* 100a).

One was supposed to accompany charity with kindness, grace, gentleness, and sympathy (*Sukk.* 49b, cf. *B.B.* 9b), and also do alms in secret.

R. Eleazar said: a Man who gives charity in secret is greater than Moses our Teacher, for of Moses it is written, *For I was afraid because of the anger and the wrath,* and of one who gives charity [secretly] it is written, *A gift in secret subdues anger (B.B. 9b).*

There is also the story told of Mar'Ukba who ran into a furnace rather than allow the recipient to know his donor (*Ket.* 67b). Poor descended from the virtuous especially were to be helped in secret (*Shek.* 5:6). However, women were not assisted in secret lest their reputation might suffer (*Hag.* 5a).

It was also considered of great importance not to delay in giving alms. Charity offerings become liable at once, not after the festivals, because the poor are waiting (*R.H.* 6a); Nahum of Gamzu's acute illness was attributed to delaying to help a poor man while he (Nahum) was unloading his ass (*Ta'an* 21a). Clouds (of the *Shekinah*) were purported to have appeared near the wife of R. Hilkiah because she gave bread rather than money to the poor so that they could be helped immediately (*Ta'an.* 23b). Further no sale was made for profit with the poor funds because a poor person might come unexpectedly and there would be nothing to give him (*Ket.* 106b), and:

R. Eleazar said in the name of R. Isaac . . . If on a fast day, the distribution of alms is postponed overnight, it is just as though blood were shed . . . This, however, applies only to bread and dates; but in the case of money, wheat or barley [postponement] does not matter (*Sanh.* 35a).

It was customary to give the money saved by fasting to the poor. *Hag* 5a reprimands those who furnish money only in the time of a person's extreme need.

Ab. 5:13 distinguishes between different types of donors:
[There are] four types of character in [respect of] almsgiving. He who desires that he [himself] should give, but that others should not give; his eye is evil towards that which appertains to others; [he who desires] that others should give, but that he [himself] should not give: his eye is evil towards that which is his [own]; he who desires [that he] himself should give, and that others should give; [he is] a pious man: [he who desires] that he himself should not give and others [too] should not give: [he is] a wicked man (*Ab.* 5:13).

Some of the biblical laws for charity, namely, the poor eating the produce of the seventh year (Exod. 23:11, cf. Lev. 25:6); the release of debts (Deut. 15:1-2); the inclusion of the poor in the pilgrim feasts (Deut. 16:11; Esther 9:22; and Neh. 8:10); the tithe of the poor in the third year (Deut. 14:28-29; 26:12-15, cf. Mal. 3:10); gifts to the poor at certain feasts (Lev. 19:9-10; 23:22; and Deut. 24:19-22); the law concerning gleanings and *pe'ah* (Lev. 19:9-10, cf. Deut. 24:19-22, cf. Ruth 2, Judg. 8:2; Isa. 24:13; and Micah 7:1); the forgotten sheaf, and the Jubilee year may have been utopian.[23]

However, over and above these the Jewish communities, especially in the Diaspora, were distinct entities.[24] It would appear that in almost all of them provisions for the poor were carefully arranged, but our information comes chiefly from the fourth to fifth centuries C. E. in Babylonia. There was the *tamhui,* the charity dish, commodities rather than money, and the *kuppah,* the charity fund. Special officers were appointed over these. They were required to have certain qualifications, and rules were attached to their functions. The charity overseers were regarded with such respect and reverence that they were permitted to marry into the priesthood without investigating any blemish in the family record (*Kidd.* 71a & 76a).

It was said that one should not put his money into a charity-bag unless it was supervised by a learned man (*A.Z.* 17b, cf. Acts 6 where the deacons are filled with wisdom and the Holy Spirit). The text

"And they turn many to righteousness as the stars for ever and ever" was accommodated to the collectors for charity (*B.B.* 8b). R. Jose said that he would prefer to collect charity rather than distribute it, because it was also difficult to perform the overseer's task with absolute impartiality (*Shabb.* 118b). The 'am ha 'aretz were not appointed to collect alms in isolation individually. If they found money in the street, they were to put it into the charity box, and if they were loaned money, they were also to place this in the charity box (*B.B.* 8b). If there were no eligible poor they must exchange the copper coins for rust-resistant ones, belonging to someone other than themselves. The overseers of the soup kitchen, if they had no poor, must sell the goods to others, not to themselves (*B.M.* 38a and *Pes.* 56a but cf. *Ark.* 6a). Or if money or food were left over from the charity fund, it was given to the poor of another city (*B.B.* 8b-9a.). No money could be taken in change either from the box of the customs-collectors or from the purse of the tax-collectors, nor could charity be taken from them, though it could be taken from their own coins which they had at home or in the marketplace.

In *B.B.* 8b one finds further details about the resources for the poor:

> Our Rabbis taught: The charity fund is collected by two persons [jointly] and distributed by three. It is collected by two, because any office conferring authority over the community must be filled by at least two persons. It must be distributed by three, on the analogy of money cases [which are tried by a Beth din of three]. Food for the soup kitchen is collected by three and distributed by three, since it is distributed as soon as it is collected. Food is distributed every day, the charity fund every Friday. The soup kitchen is for all comers, the charity fund for the poor of the town only. The townspeople, however, are at liberty to use the soup kitchen like the charity fund and vice versa, and to apply them to whatever purposes they choose (*B.B.* 8b).

Shabb. 62a mentions a woman charity overseer: she puts the seal of her signet ring on her orders for charity disbursements and wears the ring on her finger (note 1 *ad loc.*).

Everyone was liable for contributing to charity. A man who resided in a town for thirty days was liable for the soup kitchen; for three months, for the charity box; for six months, for the clothing fund; for nine months, for the burial fund; and for twelve months, for the contribution for the repair of the town walls. Even orphans were obligated to contribute, and this gave them a better social standing (*B.B.* 8a).

The person who has sufficient for two meals must not receive anything from the charity dish, and the person who has enough for fourteen meals may not receive help from the communal fund (*Pe'ah* 8:7). The *kuppah*, the communal fund, was disbursed each Friday, and provided the poor with enough for fourteen meals (cf. *Shabb.* 118a). One who has two hundred *zuzim* should not be helped by a poor man's gift, and a man was expected to sell his costlier goods before he took alms (*Ket.* 68a; *Sot.* 21b). Further it was said that the person who takes charity when he is not eligible "will not depart from this world before being actually in need of his fellow-men..." (*Pe'ah* 8:9).

The amounts given were as follows: A poor man traveling from place to place should be given not less than a loaf valued at a *pundion;* if he stays overnight, he should be given the requirements for the night, a bed and a bolster; on the Sabbath he must be given sufficient for three meals and when he departs he is provided with one meal (*Shabb.* 118a, cf. *B.B.* 9a, *Pe'ah* 8:7). Besides money for fourteen meals from the *Kuppah,* and availability of *tamhui,* the poor also received tithes. Amounts included an *'ukla* of spices, a pound of vegetables, ten nuts, five peaches, two pomegranates or one *ethrog.* From the threshing floor the poor had no less than half a *kab* of wheat, a *kab* of barley, a *kab* and a half of spelt, a *kab* of dried figs or *maneh* of pressed figs, half a *log* of wine, a quarter of oil. The quantities were obliged to be sufficient for the poor to sell the produce and procure two meals (*Er.* 29a). At the Passover even the poorest man in Israel must dine reclining, and he should be given no less than four cups of wine, even if he receives relief from the charity plate (*Pes.* 99b). Gifts were also received at *Purim.*

The dignity of the poor person was preserved very carefully. The *Shema* was recited at the time when the poor man came home to dine because he would not have artificial light (*Ber.* 2b). It is reported that R. Hana b. Hanilai had sixty cooks by day and sixty by night so that the person who was ashamed to come for sustenance during the day might come at night. Further he is purported to have kept his hand on his purse lest a respectable poor man might come, and while he was getting out his purse the recipient might put him to shame. R. Hana also threw out of his house wheat and barley so that anyone who was ashamed might come and take it by night (*Ber.* 58b). R. Abba said in the name of R. Simeon b. Lakish that he who lends money is greater than the one who performs charity, for the poor man is not ashamed to borrow, but the man who forms a contract does better, for therewith the poor can trade (*Shabb.* 63a, cf. *Ket.* 67b).[25] The secret giving of alms was also inspired by the idea that one should not embarrass a poor person (*Shabb.* 104a, cf. *Hag.* 5a).

> R. Johanan said: Concerning three things does the Holy One ... make proclamation every day (to show his approval): a bachelor who lives in a large town without sinning, a poor man who returns lost property to its owner, and a wealthy man who tithes his produce in secret (*Pes.* 113a).

It was considered a kindness to find a poor man even unnecessary work to do so that he might earn something with which to buy provisions for the Festival (*M.K.* 13a). The poor person was assisted in the dignity of mourning, for a mourner was forbidden to work for three days; thus he or she would receive maintenance from charity (*M.K.* 21b). Thereafter he did his work privately in his house, and a woman in mourning plied the spindle in her house (*M.K.* 21b). Formerly it was the custom for the rich to carry baskets of silver and gold and white glass to the house of the mourner, while the poor used osier baskets of peeled willow twigs and colored glass. However, out of deference for the poor, all were required to use the plain baskets and the colored glass (*M.K.* 27a). R. Meir said in the name of R. Ishmael that in the case of the poor, lamentation was made over a child of three and in the case of the rich, for a child of five (for the grief of the poor was greater, as children were their only joy) but R. Judah ruled five and six years respectively (*M.K.* 24b).

Further if an orphan were given in marriage she was to receive not less than fifty *zuzim* for the dowry, and if the charity funds were sufficient, she was to be fitted out in accordance with the dignity of her position (*Ket.* 67a, cf. 67b, Hillel providing a horse and a slave for a poor man). An orphan was supposed to be given a rented house, a bed, household objects, and a wife (*Ket.* 67b). An orphan girl was maintained first, and a boy afterwards, because it was unusual for a girl to go begging, and because the shame of the woman is greater than the shame of a man (*Ket.* 67a).

Further it was taught that a poor person takes priority over a rich person and also over the destitute person, for the one in utter destitution is not ashamed to ask for help, whereas the poor person may be reticent to do so. Moreover there was a difference of opinion concerning the applicants for clothing and those for food. Some said that the applicant for food is to be examined but the one for clothing is not, because without clothing he would be put to contempt (*B.B.* 9a). In addition to these needs, it was considered important not to neglect teaching for poor children (*Ned.* 81a).

With regard to the gleaning of the fields, thrice a day was considered correct at morning, noon, and sunset. "Rabban Gamaliel said that these times were set lest the poor search less often. The morning was for nursing mothers; the noon for the children who would not be awake in the morning, and sunset for the old and infirm to obtain their share before the day passes" (*Pe'ah* 4:5). One who made a distinction between one poor person and another was considered a robber (*Pe'ah* 5:6). The physician, Abba the Cupper, had a private place for people to deposit their fees so that those who could not pay would not be embarrassed (*Ta'an.* 21b). R. Akiba said that even the poor in Israel were to be considered as if they were freemen fallen into reduced circumstances, because they were all descendants of Abraham, Isaac, and Jacob (*B.K.* 90b cf. *B.M.* 8:1).

On the one hand, the poor were enabled to keep the precepts of the law; for example, the sacrificial offering was accommodated to the person's income (*Men.* 73a; *Yoma* 41a-b); one could give *demai* (untithed food) to the poor and passing troops, but they must be told that they are *demai* (Shammai ruled that they could not eat *demai;* Hillel that they could, cf. *Er.* 17a; 31a; *Pes.* 35b); a poor man was only bound to tithe each quantity if the amount was large, but not if it was small (*Demai* 5). R. Eleazar renounced a vineyard for the poor so that they could bring an offering to Jerusalem (*Bez.* 5b, cf. also *Sukk.* 44b).

On the other hand, the law was sometimes superseded in order to assist the poor. For example, they could eat of the sabbatical produce even after the time it should have been removed (*Sheb.* 8). The inhabitants of Jericho made breaches in their gardens and orchards to permit the poor to eat the fallen fruit in time of famine, on Sabbaths, and Festivals, although the sages forbade this (*Pes.* 56a). To benefit the poor, the alarm was sounded for volunteer grain even in the sabbatical year (*Ta'an.* 19b). The *Megillah* was not read on the Sabbath because the poor received gifts on the feast of Purim and they were not to be kept waiting; also, the readings were pushed forward for the same reason (*Meg.* 4b; *Ta'an.* 4b). Those who traded in the sabbatical year were persuaded to show repentance and give their profits to the poor (*Sanh.* 25b). Certain cities were not annexed to Palestine so that they could be cultivated during the sabbatical year to provide sustenance for the poor (*Hull.* 7a). Further R. Akiba said, "Treat the Sabbath like a weekday rather than be dependent on men" (*Shabb.* 118a), and R. Eleazar said, "One may determine charity [grants] to the poor on the Sabbath" (*Shabb.* 150a).

Notes

[1] I regret that I have been unable to date or to use form or redaction criticism in studying the Rabbinic material, but I hope that this collection will be of interest to readers. For a good linguistic study of the "poor," see L. C. Crockett, "The Old Testament in the Gospel of Luke," (High Wycomb, England, and Ann Arbor, Michigan, U.S.A.: University Microfilms, 1966), pp. 80-101.

[2] Martin Hengel, *Judaism and Hellenism* (Philadelphia: Fortress, 1974) I: 6.

[3] M. Rostovtzeff, *The Social and Economic History of the Ancient World*, vols. 1-3 (Oxford: Clarendon, 1926-28), p. 193.

[4] Hengel, *op. cit.*, p. 48.

[5] H. Bolkestein, *Wohltätigkeit und Armenpflege im vorchristlichen Altertum* (Utrecht, 1939).

[6] *Ibid.*, p. 42.

[7] *Ibid.*, pp. 43-44.

[8] *Ibid.*, p. 34.

[9] *Ibid.*, p. 38.

[10] Rostovtzeff, *op. cit.*, p. 129.

[11] *Ibid.*, p. 146.

[12] Hengel, *op. cit.*, p. 14.

[13] *Ibid.*, p. 26.

[14] *Ibid.*, p. 50.

[15] S. W. Baron, *A Social and Religious History of the Jews* (New York: Columbia University Press, 1958), p. 258; J. Jeremias, *Jerusalem in the Time of Jesus*, E. T. (Philadelphia: Fortress Press, 1967) *passim;* and S. Safrai & M. Stern, *The Jewish People of the First Century* (Philadelphia: Fortress Press. 1976), 2:879.

[16] Baron, *op. cit.*, p. 215, cf. also M. Hengel, *op. cit.*, vol. 1, pp. 25, 49.

[17] Cited by Baron, *op. cit.*, p. 215. However, E. Bikerman has questioned the regular payments.

[18] Rostovtzeff, *op. cit.*, pp. 230-234.

[19] Baron, *op. cit.*, p. 262.

[20] For further details see Tenny Frank, ed., *An Economic Survey of Ancient Rome, Roman Syria*, (Baltimore: John Hopkins Press, 1938) by F. M. Heichelheim, pp. 231-245, especially 239. For a later period (Herodian) see M. Safrai, *op. cit.*, vol. 1, pp. 259-60; 330-36 (in Judaea).

[21] A shield closely resembling the ones described in the War Scroll was found in Syria; cf. Y. Yadin, *The War Scroll of the Sons of Light Against the Sons of Darkness*.

[22] L. E. Keck, "The Poor Among the Saints in the New Testament," *ZNW* 56 (1965): 100-129.

[23] Bolkestein, *op. cit.*, pp. 59 and 62.

[24] V. Tcherikover, *Hellenistic Civilization and the Jews* (Paterson, N.J.: Atheneum Publishers, 1970), pp. 59 and 62.

[25] Note that this is a different policy from that of Qumran, *vida supra* pp. 44-45.

OTHER WORKS CONSULTED

Allegro, J. M. *The Treasure of the Copper Scroll*. New York: Doubleday, 1964.
Bigo, P., S. J. "La richesse comme intendance dans l' Evangile," *Nouv. Rev. Theol.* 87 (3, 1965): 267-271.
Buchanan, G. W. "Jesus and the Upper Class," *NovT* (1964), pp. 195-209.
Degenhardt, H. J. *Lukas: Evangelist der Armen*, Stuttgart, 1965.
Flusser, D. "Blessed Are the Poor in Spirit," *IEJ* 10 (1960): 1-13.
Gaechter, P. "Die Sieben," *ZKT* 74 (1952): 129-166.
Gelin, A. *The Poor of Yahweh*, Collegeville, Minn.: Liturgical Press, 1964.

Gourbillon, J. G., O. P. *Der Gott der Armen im Alten und Neuen Testament,* Düsseldorf, 1961.
Greehy, John G. "Community of Goods—Qumran and Acts," *Ir. Theo. Quart.* 65: 230-240.
Juschke, A. "Arm und reich im Alten Testament," *ZAW* 57 (1939): 31-57.
Kandler, H. J. "Die Bedeutung der Armut in Schriftum von Chirbet Qumran," *Judaica* 13 (1957): 193-211.
Leaney, A. R. C. *The Rule of Qumran and Its Meaning,* Philadelphia: Westminster Press, 1966.
Legasse, S. *L'Appel du Riche,* Paris, 1966.
Noack, B. "Jakobus wider die Reichen," *ST* 18 (1964): 10-25.
Rusche, H. "Die erwählten Armen," *Bib. u. Leb.* 11 (1970): 46-51.
Safrai, S. and M. Stern, eds., *The Jewish People in the First Century,* vol. 1, Philadelphia: Fortress Press, 1974.
Schulz, P. Anselm. "Zu einer neutestamentlichen Grundlegung der 'monastischen Armut'," *Erbe und Aftrag,* 41 (1965): 443-459.
Schürer, E. *A History of the Jewish People in the Time of Jesus,* 4 vols., Edinburgh: T & T Clark, 1890.
Stöger, Alois. "Armut und Ehelosigkeit—Besitz und Ehe der Junger nach dem Lukasevangelium," *Geist u. Leben* 40 (1967): 43-59.
Walter, N. "Zur Analyse von Mc 10:17-31," *ZNW* 53 (1962): 206-218.

6

Jesus' Personality as Reflected in His Parables

John W. Miller

Personality

The communist philosopher, Milan Machoveč, in a fascinating recent book about the Jesus of history, writes that "it is especially the twentieth century endowed with thousands of means of enriching visible human communication, which adopts the one-sided and erroneous view that what counts is *what* is said. In reality *who* is speaking is much more important, especially where there is harmony between mature words and a mature person."[1] This "one-sided and erroneous view," of which Machoveč speaks, has a definite bearing on contemporary Jesus studies. In reaction to earlier "psychologizing" tendencies in these studies, Jesus historians in recent decades have gone to the opposite extreme, stressing again and again that our sources for the life of Jesus are just too fragmentary to tell us much at all about Jesus himself. "The *character* of Jesus, the vivid picture of his personality and his life cannot now be clearly made out,"[2] insists Rudolf Bultmann in a statement typical of many that have appeared on this subject. "What is more important," he adds, is that "the content of his message is or will be ever more clearly recognizable."[3] Thus a sharp distinction is drawn between Jesus' character (who Jesus was), and his message (what he said). We can know quite a bit about the latter, it is maintained, scarcely anything about the former.

This distinction, however, is an artificial one. A man's character is revealed in his message, and even those Jesus historians who stress the impossibility of talking about Jesus in personalistic terms are themselves by no means silent on this subject. In every modern inquiry into the Jesus of history, a portrait of Jesus himself begins to emerge, and inevitably so—for how can we encounter even one sentence of a man's teaching, in our time at least, without being compelled to reflect on its personal and psychological dimensions? Thus Bultmann's "existential" Jesus,[4] or Bornkamm's Jesus of "astounding sovereignty,"[5] or the "trust"-evoking Jesus of Leander Keck,[6] to mention only three examples among many, are as clearly contributions to what John McIntyre has aptly termed a "psychological model" in Christology as any of their predecessors.[7]

What is said on this score by contemporary Jesus historians, however, is quite often short of the mark in at least two respects: (1) the personal dimensions of Jesus' life are usually not well developed in terms of historical study itself—that is, relevant material is often bypassed; and, even more significantly, (2) the personality sciences are seldom brought to bear on the subject. In short, important historical and psychological resources are neglected, and this at a time when psycho-historical study generally is a rapidly expanding field of inquiry,[8] and psychological interest in Jesus is beginning to become a pressing issue for Christian piety, theology, and apologetics.[9]

Parables

In a longer, book-length treatment of this subject which I hope to publish soon, I have reached certain conclusions about the personality of Jesus based upon a review of the literature on this subject, and a fairly comprehensive reexamination of the most reliable traditions of his life and teachings. In carrying out this investigation, I became aware of the degree to which the parables of Jesus in particular represent an important source for coming to know Jesus in the more personal sense alluded to above.

It is, of course, now widely recognized that Jesus' parables occupy a special place generally in any reconstruction of his life and teachings, for modern study has succeeded in verifying the oldest stratum of these stories as among the historically most reliable features of the Gospel traditions.[10] This has already triggered a vast outpouring of investigation into virtually every facet of the form, meaning, message, and relevance of these simple stories.[11]

As yet, however, insufficient attention has been paid to what the parables of Jesus might reveal about Jesus himself. An exception is Etienne Trocmé,[12] who has argued that most of these stories were first spoken in the setting of meals, and were in fact initially remembered and passed along by Jesus' middle-class Jewish hosts. As such, he writes, they point to Jesus as a much-admired guest and conversationalist, and the impression he made on a group that was socially and economically closer to him than any other. Whether or not this hypothesis is correct, parables peopled by as rich a gallery of personalities as, for the most part, Jesus' stories are, must surely tell us something about the outlook and personality of their author.

I can only hope, in this short article, dedicated to my friend and one-time colleague, Howard Charles, to give a few illustrations of the kinds of things I have in mind in making this point.

Motivation

Since the beginning of modern Gospel studies, in the latter part of the eighteenth century, the question as to what really motivated the Jesus of history at the time of his public mission has been at the forefront of the quest of the historical Jesus.[13] The traditional notion that he was bent upon promoting himself and his own messianic dignity, which was such a contentious point in the psychiatric study of Jesus at the beginning of this century,[14] has by now pretty well been abandoned. Biblical scholars generally agree that it is open to doubt that Jesus appropriated to himself any of the traditional Christological titles (Messiah, Son of God, Son of Man).[15] Another reality claimed him: the nearness of God's kingdom (Mark 1:14f.). Furthermore, there is considerable unity as well as to what he might have meant by these enigmatic words. A new age was dawning, one that would soon reach its consummation, but was already manifesting itself in the here and now.[16] This he saw happening wherever "by the finger of God" (Luke 11:20) exorcism, healing, and spiritual renewal were occurring among the poor, the lost, the little ones, and the spiritually disenfranchised generally.[17] We now realize that many, perhaps most, of the parables of Jesus were originally spoken to either evoke, explain, or defend his belief that God was moving in compassion among the "lost sheep of the house of Israel," bringing them back to himself. "Be merciful, even as your Father is merciful" (Luke 6:36). The tact (Luke 7:41-43), firmness (Matt. 20:1-16), and persistence (Luke 15:4-32) with which his parables suggest he went about doing this, alert us to the degree to which he was committed to the task of proclaiming "good news to the poor" (Matt. 11:5), and winning a place for them in the household of Israel's God. "Those who are well have no need of a physician, but those who are sick; I came not to call the righteous, but sinners" (Mark 2:17). The parables of Jesus thus lend credibility to the point of view of Jeremias that Jesus' entire ministry was bent upon establishing the eschatological people of God as a community of grace.[18] But how, more specifically, might we characterize someone who aims at something of this magnitude?

Character

A man is revealed, in part, by the friends he keeps, but also by his opponents. In the people who appear in Jesus' parables, it might be argued, we meet some of his friends and opponents as he viewed them. In any case, many of his stories are dominated by a dual set of figures, one of whom might be termed "heroic," the other antagonist, adversary, or "villain," providing we do not forget that the "villains" too, in these stories, are invariably portrayed in a friendly manner.

Looking at these "villains" first of all, what can be said of them individually and as a group? Examples range from the Pharisee at prayer, who thanked God that he was not like other men (Luke 18:9-13) to the grumbling workers, jealous because their co-workers were being treated generously (Matt. 20:12), to the forgiven debtor who treats an underling with impunity (Matt. 18:23ff.), the priest and the Levite who walked by on the other side (Luke 10:29-37), the son who said a courteous "Yes, sir . . ." when his father asked him to work in his vineyard, but then procrastinated (Matt. 21:31), the men who made petty excuses when it was time for attending a banquet to which they had previously committed themselves (Luke 14:16ff.), the unbending elder brother (Luke 15:11-32), the irresponsible servant (Luke 12:42-46), the timid, sullen investor (Matt. 25:14-30). The list could easily be extended, but this much already reveals that the "villains" come from every social class and walk in life, but bear a common visage. They are all on the snobbish side—hard working for the most part, self-righteous, careful about appearances, but not at all ready to take risks. If Jesus did not like these qualities in others, it stands to reason that he did not like them in himself, and was not this kind of person.

If we ask, on the other hand, who represents Jesus in these parables, there are at least two instances where the answer would appear to be especially apparent: the parables of the prodigal son (Luke 15:11-32), and the generous employer (Matt. 20:1-16). In both instances, these stories come to their climax and close with some very sharply worded speeches aimed at their "opponents," and urging them to alter their attitude toward those who are the recipients of some rather excessive "generosity." Without doubt Jesus himself is speaking through the mouth of the father in the story of the prodigal son, and through the mouth of the employer in the parable of the generous employer. "Are you jealous because I am generous?" the latter asks at the close of his reprimand to his complaining employees. These then are Jesus' "heroes," and in both instances one might legitimately characterize them as strong, competent, in-charge, self-determined "father figures," but with a definite eccentricity. They are, or can be, unpredictably compassionate. They give parties for sons who have scarcely repented, and pay a whole day's wages to men who have worked only one hour.

Comparable types recur in the parables: the shepherd who impulsively leaves his flock in the wilderness to fend for itself while he frantically searches for the one sheep that is lost (Luke 15:4-7); the pearl merchant who wagers all on a single gem (Matt. 13:45f.); the farmer who refused to panic in the face of an overgrowth of weeds (Matt. 13:24-30); the steward who worked out an alternative plan, on the spot, when his job was threatened (Luke 16:1-9a); the merchant who put his money to work for him before going abroad (Matt. 25:14-30); the blunt, straight-talking "father" Abraham (Luke 16:19-31); the superbly benevolent Samaritan (Luke 10:29-37); the super-forgiving king (Matt. 18:23-35). Can it be doubted that collectively these "heroes" reflect and refract significant facets of Jesus' own personality: his competence, his intelligence, his candor, his daring, his realism, his patience, his impulsiveness, his firmness, his compassion?

Manner

But the parables reveal still more. They not only enrich our impression of his character, they indicate something of his manner and mood as well—a facet of his personality that has not generally been accorded the attention it deserves. And yet "the characteristic thing about him," writes Henry J. Cadbury, "may well have been rather the manner than the matter of his thinking."[19]

That Jesus delighted in parables is itself worth pondering in this respect. Clearly these stories were not "adduced . . . to confirm insights independently arrived at."[20] Parables, rather, must have been his typical mode of thinking, the way he grasped truth and was grasped by it.[21] That being the case, it is especially striking that not a single story has to do with Scripture (Torah), as do many of the parables of his Rabbinic contemporaries.[22] His focus is elsewhere, on nature and the nitty-gritty of daily affairs. Life itself, one might say, was his bible, and he seems to have read it from a very unique angle.

What angle? "If you then, who are evil," he once said, "know how to give good gifts to your children, how much more will your Father who is in heaven give good things to those who ask him?" (Matt. 7:11). Again and again in the parables we seem to encounter this "how much more," either explicitly or implicitly, a fact which prompted Henry Cadbury to write that there seems to be something of a quantitative feature in Jesus' thought. "He does not hesitate to infer that what man does God also will do, or will be even more likely to do . . ."[23] For example Jesus asks, what man, asleep in bed at midnight, would respond to the entreaty of a friend for bread by brusquely sending him away (Luke 11:5ff.)? Why, even if he were not much of a friend, would he not rather get up and give it, if for no other reason than his friend's importunity? Well then, he implies, how much more can we count on God to respond to our needs and prayers (cp. Luke 18:6f.). Or look at the tiny mustard seed, which falls on the ground, germinates, and grows into a large bush in one season (Luke 13:18f.). If things like this are happening all around us, how much more . . . God's kingdom. "Possibly Jesus himself regularly thought in such terms," adds Cadbury. "Whether by induction or by illustration, spiritual truth came to him in close association with observable data of outward life."[24] Or as Trocmé puts it: ". . . many of the parables radiate an extraordinary atmosphere, which is all the more striking in that it penetrates the most commonplace events of life and transfigures them without suppressing them."[25]

If we were to try to characterize this mental outlook more precisely, would it be wrong to say that Jesus was an optimist? He lived in one of the darkest, most tragic eras of Jewish history. Many of his contemporaries were locked in the grip of a fanatical despair that would eventually lead to militant uprisings and a suicidal clash with Rome. But of all this there is virtually nothing in his parables. In a time like that Jesus was not looking on the dark side. He was looking at how things grow, at the gracious and forgiving way fathers sometimes treat their wayward sons, at the way employers sometimes overpay their poor employees, and kings forgive their incompetent subjects and servants, at the way the sun keeps shining and the rain falling on good and bad alike (Matt. 5:45). And from all this he drew the most remarkably positive conclusions about God and life in general.

A clue as to why may be found in still a third observation: what the parables tell us about Jesus' sense of humor. The traditional image of Jesus is tragically flawed at this point.[26] He is generally pictured as somber, almost morose, a man of sorrows and acquainted with grief. Studying the earliest versions of his stories, however, has convinced more than one modern student of the parables that this is a distortion.[27] In parable after parable there are twists and turns that make us smile, and sometimes laugh out loud. It is amusing, for example, the way the wicked judge (Luke 18:1-8) admits to himself that it is actually quite true, as Jesus has just said, that he is a wicked fellow who neither fears God nor regards his fellowmen. But yet what is he to do? A man's got to live, doesn't he? So, lest this widow here wears him out with her continual coming, well, he'll just have to compromise and do something good for a change! The rationalizations that men give for their actions in these stories are often ludicrous (Luke 14:16-24).

"What am I going to do?" ponders the impossibly irresponsible farm manager, even as his employer is getting ready to give him the boot. "I'm no longer strong enough to dig, and I'm ashamed to beg" (Luke 16:3). The "friend" in the parable of the friend at midnight (Luke 11:5-8) blusters behind the locked door that he is in bed with his children, and will not get up, bread or no bread, friend or no friend. "Do not bother me!" When the servant in the parable of the unmerciful servant (Matt. 18:23-35) finds out that he is in debt to the tune of a sum approximating the annual budget of the Roman Empire, he throws himself to the ground and promises to pay all! "O God, I thank thee that I am not like other men . . ." postures the Pharisee at prayer (Luke 18:11).

What is humor? There is humor at other people's expense (sarcasm, satire); there is dirty humor (glimpsing the forbidden); there is humor that helps us confront the foibles and failures of life, by not taking them too seriously. Imperfections or failures in themselves are not humorous. They become humorous when they are handled in such a way that "we can enjoy the fact that failure is not a sign of fatal disaster."[28] This, as Jacob Jonsson has rightly seen, is the humor of Jesus. Think again, in this light, of Jesus' portrait of the wicked judge. He may in fact have had reason, in the course of his life, to think rather bitterly of such unjust and capricious authorities. But in his parable Jesus captures this man in a rare moment of perplexity when he is contemplating doing good in spite of himself. In the glow of this quixotic possibility we forget momentarily his moral failures. Even Jesus' portrait of the Pharisee at prayer might be viewed, in this light, as in-group teasing rather than satirical put-down, if we remember the degree to which Jesus shared the essence of this man's religious point of view (Luke 15:31).

In any case a man who can handle reality in this way must have had a very positive outlook on life, but not, we must now emphasize, because he hides his face from all the foolishness and moral confusion that abound in the world. Rather he sees all that, but still insists on trusting, on believing that not even the worst of men, or the worst of times, are totally bad, nor the best of them totally good. Under all and over all is the goodness of God. "No one is good but God alone" (Mark 10:18).

Background

How did Jesus become the man he was at thirty (Luke 3:23)? With this question we come close to the concerns that have preoccupied modern psychology since Freud. Just as a nation may achieve self-understanding through historical inquiry, so individuals may gain self-understanding through personal knowledge of their past. Modern psychology teaches that we become what we are as adults, through well-marked developmental stages from birth onward. Jesus too "increased in wisdom and in stature, and in favor with God and man" (Luke 2:52). "He learned obedience through what he suffered" (Hebrews 5:8). A fuller understanding of what this might have entailed, in his case, is becoming an increasingly important field of investigation for anyone interested in arriving at a modern Christology. "Once we agree," writes Gerald O'Collins, "that as a geniune human being Jesus developed psychologically, we cannot then ignore Freud, Jung, and Erikson by refusing even to raise the question: What could that development have been like—before and after puberty?"[29]

Unfortunately historically reliable traditions concerning Jesus' life prior to his public ministry are minimal, a fact that permitted very free play of imagination and the proliferation of some rather bizarre infancy Gospels already in the first Christian centuries. Although initially popular, these first sketches of Jesus' childhood are today justifiably rejected out of hand as of little or no value.[30] But it cannot be said that the need that gave rise to these narratives does not persist, and increasingly so in a time like ours when there is a growing awareness of the importance of the childhood years for the shape of adult personality. Did Jesus have a happy childhood? What about his relations with his mother, his father, his siblings? What schooling did he have? Who were his friends? How widely did he travel? What was his occupation? Did he marry? If not, why not? Hypothetical answers to questions of this nature will inevitably shape themselves in our minds. More often than not, however, they will remain implicit rather than explicit. I proceed on the assumption that an explicit hypothesis is better than a covert one, and a good one better than a bad one.

The parables themselves do not supply us with the hard data necessary for constructing such a hypothesis. For that we must rely on data, sparse as it might be, from elsewhere in the Gospels. In Luke 2:7 and Mark 6:3, for example, we learn that Jesus was the firstborn in a family that eventually included four brothers and several sisters. These same texts tell us that as an adult he worked in carpentry, as his father before him had done (Matt. 13:55). Since there is no reference to a wife or family of his own, it is generally assumed that he was celibate, and remained so until the time of his public ministry. Only then did he move out of his parental home to a house of his own in Capernaum (Mark 2:15, 3:19b). The fact that his father is nowhere mentioned during his public career suggests that he might have died before Jesus' thirtieth year.[31] If so, this death might have occurred in Jesus' early adolescence and explains why he never married (see below).

If the parables are deficient in factual data regarding his developmental years, however, they do allow us to amplify these few hints by giving us a rather rich visual impression of his world, his vocational orientation, and his experience of family life generally.

(1) First of all, a few comments about the *world* in which Jesus grew to manhood, as this is reflected in these stories. Looking at the parables with this in mind, one is struck, first of all, by the *social diversity* of the scenes portrayed there. Not just one world shows up in these parables, but many worlds. Artistic representations of Jesus usually picture him against a background of village or field. And, to be sure, this side of Palestinian life is richly evident in the stories he told. But there are city scenes there as well. If there are shepherds and farmers, there are also kings and judges. If there are men sowing their fields, there are also merchants busy with buying and selling. If there are villagers knocking on neighbors' doors at midnight for three loaves of bread, there are also wealthy moneylenders about to take off for distant places. And what is equally surprising, once one notices all this, is the ease with which Jesus passes from one scene to another. He seems to be equally at home in all of them.

Perhaps Jesus was a more cosmopolitan figure than we have traditionally thought him to be.[32] At the same time it is worth noting that his parables are remarkably void of references to history or world affairs:

> There is a hereness and nowness about his language, a preoccupation with the scene right in front of him. He recalls, of

course, a few episodes from biblical history or myth like the story of the flood and the destruction of Sodom. But Jesus portrays little interest in the past. He never mentions that founding event of Jewish history, the exodus from Egypt. The Maccabean revolt, the Hasmonean period, the capture of Jerusalem by Pompey, the switch of Jewish allegiance to Julius Caesar, the reign of Herod the Great (37-4 B.C.) and all the other crowded events of recent history never even got a passing nod in Jesus' preaching. That larger world of politics fails to come in sight. Apart from a brief remark about paying taxes to Caesar and a comment on some victims of Pilate's brutality, Jesus hardly even suggests that he is living under Roman rule.... He neither scans history, not even the most recent history, nor lets his eye run around the Roman Empire for images and examples that he could press into service.[33]

So far as his social world was concerned, then, Jesus was no small-town provincial, obviously. On the contrary his parables suggest that he moved in and out of many circles. At the same time history and public affairs in the wider Roman Empire did not seem to interest him.

(2) The parables can possibly shed some light as well on the *work* that Jesus did during his so-called "preparatory" years. The reference in Mark 6:3 to his being a carpenter has usually been taken to mean that he worked as a *village* carpenter, fashioning plows, yokes, pitchforks, doors, windows, household furniture and the like. Artists generally have imagined him to be rather poor and working alone in simple surroundings, by himself, or with his father, Joseph.

If the parables surprise us by their cosmopolitanism, they surprise us even more by their consistently middle-class atmosphere.[34] If Jesus was in fact a poor man, working alone in a village carpenter shop, this facet of his life has failed to register itself in the stories that he told. Neither village carpenters, nor their handiwork, show up in these stories at all. We encounter instead owners of vineyards who at harvest time must worry about hiring and paying large numbers of laborers (Matt. 20:1-16); fathers with substantial wealth to be distributed (Luke 15:11-32); wealthy traveling tradesmen (Luke 10:29-37; Matt. 13:45f.); farmers with servants (Matt. 24:45-51; 13:24-30); businessmen with surplus capital to worry about (Matt. 25:14-30); rich entrepreneurs (Luke 16:1-9a), and powerful kings (Matt. 18:23-35). Even the shepherd referred to has a substantial flock of a hundred sheep (Matt. 18:12-14). Only the women in these stories are poor (Luke 15:8-10; 18:1-8), and this apparently because they are widows.

Did Jesus, in the decades prior to his public ministry, belong to the lower class or poor as we generally think? Was he even a carpenter? George Buchanan has suggested that 2 Corinthians 8:9 ("For you know the grace of our Lord Jesus Christ, that though he was rich, yet for your sake he became poor . . .") might well refer to the Jesus of history. [35] Prior to his public mission, Buchanan argues, Jesus was more like a "contractor" than a village carpenter. As such he would have employed and managed other men, and built on a larger scale. In one of his parables Jesus asked whether a man who is going to build a tower will not first do a cost analysis to find out whether the funds are available to complete the project (Luke 14:28). And in constructing a house, he says in another place, it is only the foolish builder who does not pay close attention to the foundation, whether it is on rock or on soil that can be washed away when a torrent of rain falls and there is flooding (Luke 6:47-49). A man who talks like this does in fact sound more like a building contractor, than a craftsman in wood only. In any case it is striking how many of the parables reflect a "managerial" point of view. By and large, the men in Jesus' parables are people of substance wrestling with what to do in the face of problems that typically confront those in positions of responsibility. Even the so-called good Samaritan is remarkable for his ability to handle a crisis and think through all that will be needed to help the man who fell among thieves get back on his feet again—down to the point of taking care of his hotel expenses on his return visit to that area.

The impression grows that Jesus was not only a man of his times, a cosmopolitan, as suggested above, a businessman of sorts, but, of course, more than a businessman.

(3) There is a third facet of Jesus' background reflected in the parables, perhaps the most crucial one of all, so far as his personality is concerned: his experience of family. In the light of what we now know of the effect of interpersonal relations within the family for the emotional well-being of a child, the question as to how Jesus may have fared at this point is both legitimate, as already intimated, and important for a well-thought-through twentieth century Christology. How, for example, did Jesus experience that period in life when it is mandatory for a son to break the tie with his mother and establish a positive identification with his father (the so-called Oedipal years from three to six)? Several decades ago already R. S. Lee came to the Gospels with this question in mind and concluded

that Jesus' warm evocation of God as father and his relaxed attitude toward the reality of the world, so strikingly displayed in his parables, give ample proof of an exemplary development at this point.[36]

It is apparent, however, that, like all of us, Jesus' passage to maturity was not without its testings and crises. I have already referred to the possibility that his father died prior to his public ministry. If so, and if Jesus were not married, as eldest son responsibility for his deceased father's family would have fallen on his shoulders. This would in turn have plunged him into the emotionally demanding role of surrogate husband and father in his father's own family. As suggested above, these tragic events may have transpired early in Jesus' teenage years before he had reached the age when normally his father would have found him a wife. Otherwise it would be difficult to explain why Joseph was delinquent in this most crucial of the traditional responsibilities of a Jewish father toward his son, and this his firstborn son at that.[37] I cannot therefore agree with Phipps, who argues that, given the prevailing emphasis on the importance of marriage, it is unthinkable that Jesus too was not married.[38] Everything we know contradicts this, including some hints from the parables which I will mention shortly. But this does not mean that Jesus knew nothing about the trials and tribulations of heading up a home. His personal experience of this important dimension of life was gained, however, as leader in the home of his deceased father, not in a home of his own.

The parables confirm this hypothesis. I have already mentioned the gallery of competent, compassionate "father figures" put before us there, and have suggested that they might well reflect the personality of Jesus himself. If that is true, one might legitimately ask how Jesus arrived at such a "fatherly" orientation and experience of life, if he himself never married, or had no children of his own? His role as surrogate father in his deceased father's family is a possible answer.

And this possibility is enhanced when we take note of the fact that the "fathers" in Jesus' parables are in every instance pictured alone and without wives. It is remarkable in general how few women there are in these stories, but even the few that are mentioned, as already noted, are explicitly (Luke 18:1-8) or presumably (Luke 15:8-10) widowed. There is not a single parable where a husband and his wife, a wife and her husband, play a role together.

Is this an accident? Perhaps, but there are several parables where the silence at this point is tangible. Why, for example, does the man, in the parable of the friend at midnight shout from behind his locked door, "Do not bother me; the door is now shut, and *my children* are with me in bed . . ." (Luke 11:7)? Does this man have no wife? And where is the mother of the prodigal son? Is she not overjoyed as well as her husband at the lost son's return? "He defends married life," writes Gerald O'Collins, "by rejecting divorce, and insisting that even in their minds men should not go lusting after other men's wives. He speaks of marriage feasts, wedding guests, and the maidens who waited for the bridegroom to fetch his bride from her parents' home to his own. But there the imagery stops. Nothing survives from the preaching of Jesus about the loving and caring life together of married people."[39]

How are we to explain this? Jesus' references to early childhood suggest that for him the first years of his life were happy ones, perhaps even idyllic. Otherwise how could he have said, "Truly, I say to you, whoever does not receive the kingdom of God like a child shall not enter it" (Mark 10:15). How too, were this not the case, could he have addressed God so endearingly as *Abba,* a word whose emotional home is the warm and trusting bond fashioned early in life between a son and his father? But if Jesus' childhood was a happy one, then it seems equally evident that his adolescence was tragic because of his father's death. It is for this reason, I hypothesize, that he remained in his parental home, shouldering the responsibilities that fell upon him there, and never married. In the providence of God, however, it was precisely this tragedy, with all of its attendant challenges and opportunities, which was to prepare him for his mission at thirty when, coming from Jordan's murky waters, the heavens opened, and a voice said: "Thou art my beloved Son; with thee I am well pleased" (Mark 1:11). Soon thereafter he became the center of a growing movement which, on more than one occasion, he spoke of as his true family (Mark 3:34f.).

Generativity

I began this admittedly fragmentary overview of the personality of Jesus, as reflected in his parables, by noting the degree to which these stories portray him as a man intent upon doing something to help his people Israel. I have concluded it by pointing to evidence that would intimate that there was a preparatory background to this mission in Jesus' experience within his parental family. Long before Jesus launched out in a ministry to "the lost sheep of the house of Israel," he was deeply engaged in heavy responsibilities within his own family, and very much a part of the trials and tribulations of the life of first century Palestine.

Tradition has emphasized the divine Jesus; the miracle-working Jesus; the serious, rebuking, summoning Jesus; Jesus the crucified, resurrected, and now ruling, cosmic Lord. In the parables we meet the human Jesus; the down-to-earth Jesus; Jesus the storyteller; Jesus the man of God who believes that a new age is dawning; Jesus the optimist, the humorist, the man of village and city; the mature Jesus; the joyful, competent, decisive, intelligent, candid, daring, caring, realistic, impulsive, firm, and compassionate Jesus, who is moved by the return of a wayward son to his father, but has little to say about mothers or wives; the middle-class, managerial Jesus; Jesus the guardian of his deceased father's family; Jesus the carpenter-contractor, who knows about building towers and houses, but who has left behind his family and profession, and is now at work on the spiritual foundations of the tottering household of Israel.

Modern psychology has given us yet another name for such a man, one that might well be added to the array of Christological honors that have been heaped upon him. A man who has surmounted the developmental challenges of early childhood and adolescence, who has garnered from his relation to his mother, "trust"; from his bond with his father, "self-identity"; and from his growing involvement with the world at large, "competence," may at maturity become a "generative man," writes Erik Erikson in his famous essay, "Eight Ages of Man."[40] By this he refers to someone capable of "caring" and "taking care of," someone able to take responsibility for that which has been "generated," beginning with children. And "the true saints," adds Erikson, in another study,[41] "are those who transfer the state of householdership to the house of God, becoming father and mother, brother and sister, son and daughter, to all creation, rather than to their own issue" alone.

It was, of course, in no ordinary sense that Jesus did this, but as a unique individual uniquely guided and sustained by God at an unparalleled turning point in the history of the Jewish people and the world.[42] His courage in facing the peculiar temptations and testings that beset him personally, and his integrity in responding to the call of God when it came to win "sinners" to repentance, and a fresh sense of at-homeness in the household of God (1 Tim. 1:15), set in motion redemptive forces that quickly burst the bounds of Judaism and overflowed into the wider stream of the Roman Empire, and subsequently of the world. And the end to what he began is still not in sight.

What is in sight—and this alone is the point of this inquiry—are the personal qualities of the man himself, now as always a Savior to those who look to him with love and respect, and seek to follow in his steps.

Notes

[1] Milan Machoveč, *A Marxist Looks at Jesus* (Philadelphia: Fortress Press, 1976), p. 79.

[2] Rudolf Bultmann and Karl Kundsin, *Form Criticism, Two Essays on New Testament Research* (New York: Harper & Row, 1934), p. 61.

[3] *Ibid.*, p. 61.

[4] "Fundamental in the thought of Jesus is the conception of man as a being whose every action arises out of intention, out of will." Rudolf Bultmann, *Jesus and the Word* (New York: Charles Scribner & Sons, 1958), p. 174.

[5] Günther Bornkamm, *Jesus of Nazareth* (New York: Harper & Row, 1960), p. 58.

[6] Leander Keck, *A Future for the Historical Jesus* (Nashville and New York: Abingdon, 1971), especially the section entitled, "Salvation by Trust in Jesus," pp. 177 ff.

[7] John McIntyre, *The Shape of Christology* (London: SCM, 1966), pp. 114ff.

[8] For a review of the literature, see especially Bruce Mazlish, editor, *Psychoanalysis and History,* revised edition (New York: Grosset & Dunlap, Inc., 1971); also, Roger Johnson, editor, *Psychohistory and Religion, The Case of Young Man Luther* (Philadelphia: Fortress, 1977).

[9] On this point Gerald O'Collins, S. J., in his book, *What Are They Saying about Jesus?* (New York: Paulist Press, 1977), p. 15 writes: "Christology 'from below' takes place in a world of thought that has been led in new directions by Darwin, Marx, Freud, Durkheim, John Stuart Mill and a host of other pioneers. The human sciences have taught us all to appreciate man in his many-faceted sociological, psychological and political dimensions. Theologians can hardly be expected to forget all this schooling once they turn to consider Jesus of Nazareth: It would be schizoid to inhabit one world as a result of one's seminary training and another world as a result of one's university studies."

[10] Joachim Jeremias, *The Parables of Jesus,* revised edition, (London: SCM, 1963), is widely regarded as the single most important contribution to this development.

[11] For a comprehensive bibliography, see John Dominic Crossan, "A Basic Bibliography for Parables Research," *Semeia* 1 (1974), pp. 236-274.

[12] Etienne Trocmé, *Jesus as Seen by His Contemporaries* (Philadelphia: Westminster, 1973), pp. 81 ff. esp. p. 91.

[13] The pioneering essay by Reimarus, "On the Intentions of Jesus and His Disciples," first published in 1778, has recently been republished under the title, *Reimarus: Fragments,* edited by Charles Talbert (Philadelphia: Fortress, 1970).

[14] For a review of this controversy, see Albert Schweitzer, *The Psychiatric Study of Jesus* (Boston: Beacon Press, 1948).

[15] For a fresh and provocative review of this much discussed issue, see Geza Vermes, *Jesus the Jew* (London: William Collins Sons, 1973).

[16] For documentation see especially Joachim Jeremias, *New Testament Theology,* vol. I, *The Proclamation of Jesus,* pp. 76 ff. David Flusser, a Jewish scholar, writes that Jesus "is the only Jew of ancient times known to us, who preached not only that men were on the threshold of the end time, but that the new

age of salvation had already begun." *Jesus* (New York: Herder & Herder, 1969), p. 90.

[17] Jeremias, *The Proclamation of Jesus*, pp. 108 ff.

[18] *Ibid.*, pp. 170-178. Jeremias's discussion of this issue, however, would appear to be strongly influenced by his German Lutheran presuppositions, and thus is in need of careful appraisal and testing by scholars from other confessional backgrounds.

[19] Henry J. Cadbury, *Jesus, What Manner of Man* (New York: Macmillan, 1947), p. vi.

[20] *Ibid.*, p. 53.

[21] Major attention is devoted to this facet of Jesus' thought in John Dominic Crossan's *In Parables, The Challenge of the Historical Jesus* (New York: Harper & Row, 1973).

[22] "The Rabbis said, 'Let not the parable be a small thing in your eyes, for through a parable a man can attain to understanding of the Torah.'" See Eta Linnemann, *Parables of Jesus, Introduction and Exposition* (London: S.P.C.K., 1966), p. 19.

[23] Cadbury, *Jesus, What Manner of Man*, p. 21.

[24] *Ibid.*, p. 21.

[25] Trocmé, *Jesus as Seen by His Contemporaries*, p. 95.

[26] On this theme see Elton Trueblood, *The Humor of Christ* (New York: Harper & Row, 1964); and Jakob Jonsson, *Humour and Irony in the New Testament* (Reykjavik, 1965).

[27] David Granskou, *Preaching on the Parables* (Philadelphia: Fortress Press, 1972), has especially emphasized this facet of the parables.

[28] Jakob Jõnsson, *op. cit.*, p. 18.

[29] Gerald O'Collins, *What Are They Saying About Jesus?*, p. 15.

[30] The earliest and most widely circulating of these accounts of Jesus' childhood, "The Infancy Gospel of Thomas" (recently republished in *Sourcebook of Texts for the Comparative Study of the Gospels*, edited by D. L. Dungan and D. R. Cartledge, SBL, 1973), merits careful study for what it tells us about the psychological orientation of the groups who produced and enjoyed it.

[31] "It is almost certain that Jesus' father died before Jesus was baptized. He may have died when Jesus was still quite a child." D. Flusser, *Jesus*, p. 17.

[32] In an article on "Sepphoris—Seat of the Galilean Sanhedrin," *Explor, A Journal of Theology*, Winter (1977): 36-43, Francis Boelter suggests that a new appraisal of Jesus' possible contacts with this major Galilean city, located just three miles from Nazareth, is needed. Herod Antipas had his royal residence there until the building of Tiberius (c. A.D. 18), and the city was the scene of major building projects during Jesus' growing up years.

[33] Gerald O'Collins, *op. cit.*, pp. 71f.

[34] Trocmé, *Jesus as Seen by His Contemporaries*, pp. 91 ff.

[35] George Wesley Buchanan, "Jesus and the Upper Classes," *Novum Testamentum*, VII (1964-65): 195-209.

[36] R. S. Lee, *Freud and Christianity* (Penguin Books, 1948), especially pp. 166 ff.

[37] In the Talmud it is said that a father has five principal responsibilities to his son: He must circumcise him, redeem him, teach him Torah, teach him a trade, and find him a wife. (Kiddushin 29a). See on this William Phipps, *Was Jesus Married?* (New York: Harper & Row, 1970), p. 47.

[38] William Phipps, *The Sexuality of Jesus* (New York: Harper & Row, 1973).

[39] Gerald O'Collins, *op. cit.*, pp. 68 f.

[40] Erik Erikson, "Eight Ages of Man," *Childhood and Society*, second edition (New York: W. W. Norton & Co., Inc., 1963). On the contemporary importance of "generativity" as an ethical ideal, see Don Browning, *Generative Man: Psychoanalytic Perspectives* (Philadelphia: Westminster, 1973).

[41] Erik Erikson, *Gandhi's Truth: On the Origins of Militant Nonviolence* (New

York: W. W. Norton & Co., Inc., 1969), p. 399.

[42] On this way of viewing Jesus see Michael Goulder's essay, "Jesus, the Man of Universal Destiny," in *The Myth of God Incarnate,* edited by John Hick (Philadelphia: Westminster Press, 1978).

7

The Structural Function of the Term 'Way' (*Hodos*) in Mark's Gospel

Willard M. Swartley

Professor Howard Charles, through his use of the inductive method of Bible study in teaching New Testament book studies at Goshen Biblical Seminary, has greatly enriched the Bible study methods of many pastors and teachers in the Mennonite Church. As one of his students, I am greatly indebted to Professor Charles for his style of study, teaching, and fostering of learning, a style I have tried to use in my own study and teaching of the Bible. In the year after my graduation, this method bore fruit in my discovery of germinal insights into the structural organization of Mark's Gospel.[1] This article is an outgrowth of those initial insights.

The inductive method of Bible study makes a careful observation of the text the foundation of all interpretation. This observation focuses especially on the structural features of the text. The approach is holistic; it takes the text in its canonical form and derives its clues for finding the author's purpose and for interpretation from a thorough structural or compositional analysis of the text. The inductive (structural) method as taught by Professor Charles has been extensively described by Robert A. Traina in his book, *Methodical Bible Study*.[2]

In the last decade, other varieties of structural method have emerged in biblical studies. The current exegetical method or hermeneutic known as structuralism builds upon assumptions and methods that both resemble and differ from the method taught by Professor Charles and reflected in this article.[3]

The style of biblical study exemplified by Professor Charles includes more than method, however. Dedication to teaching, reverence for the biblical text, and patient perseverance in the learning process are personal and pedagogical virtues remembered and cherished by his students. I am happy to dedicate this article to Howard Charles, my esteemed teacher and beloved brother.

This study limits itself to an investigation of the structural function of the term *way (hodos)* in Mark's Gospel, especially as it is used in Mark 8:27-10:52 and in the opening verses, 1:2, 3. The discussion will focus on five closely related objectives:

1. To summarize briefly the current widely accepted redactional emphases in Mark 8:27-10:52.
2. To examine the use of *hodos* in both 8:27-10:52 and 1:2, 3.
3. To summarize scholarly views on the significance of Mark's use of *hodos*.
4. To propose that Mark's structural design for 8:27-10:52 incorporates the discipleship motif into another structural framework wherein *hodos* functions as a representation of Israel's way to the promised land (transposed now to "the kingdom of God").
5. To suggest basic motifs and perspectives which Mark's *hodos* theology can contribute to our understanding of Christian thought and life.

I. Redactional Emphases of 8:27-10:52

Markan scholars generally recognize that the three predominant themes in 8:27-10:52 are anticipation of Jesus' passion, teaching on Jesus' messiahship, and teaching on discipleship. It is likewise recognized that the teaching is presented via a careful structural pattern: three passion predictions (8:31; 9:31; 10:32f), followed by three failures of the disciples to understand (8:32-33; 9:32; 10:35-41), followed in turn by three sessions where Jesus teaches discipleship (8:34-38; 9:35-37; 10:42-45).[4] Discussion of the passion predictions lies outside the scope of this study. On this matter, see Georg Strecker's discussion of the passion predictions in Mark's Gospel.[5]

Three features accent Mark's teaching on messiahship: the placement of christological declarations at both the opening and ending of the section (Peter's confession and Bartimaeus's acclamation respectively), the recurring use of the title Son of Man, and the heavenly voice declaring Jesus' sonship upon the mount of transfiguration. Helpful discussion of Mark's christological intentions may be found in numerous articles, notably in essays by Norman Perrin[6] and Philipp Vielhauer.[7]

The widely recognized Markan emphasis that 8:27-10:52 concentrates upon Jesus' teaching on discipleship has been further supported by the studies of Konrad Weiss[8] and Quentin

Quesnell.[9] Weiss classifies all the pericopae in this section of Mark's Gospel under the categories of narrative and teaching. He concludes that even the narrative materials contain didactic elements; thus "the whole is an instruction guide for the disciples, ("das Ganze ist 'Jüngerunterweisung')."[10]

Quesnell's study shows that this section of Mark's Gospel contains an unusually high percentage of material devoted to the words of Jesus. Fifty-nine percent of the material is given to *words* of Jesus as compared to forty-six percent in the entire Gospel and forty-one percent in the preceding section (6:30-8:26).[11] Quesnell further observes that whereas in the entire Gospel preceding 8:27 only two statements of universal moral directive occur (3:29, 35), in 8:27-10:52 twenty-three didactic statements of universal moral directive occur.[12]

Indeed, Mark's redactional emphases upon messiahship and discipleship in 8:27-10:52 have been widely discussed and the aim of this paper is not to linger longer on these matters. The distinctive Markan feature which merits more attention than it has received in scholarly study is Mark's frequent and striking use of the term *way (hodos)* throughout this section of the Gospel. To this point, this study will now direct its focus.

II. Mark's Use of 'Way' (*Hodos*) in 8:27-10:52

Mark uses the term *hodos* seven times in 8:27-10:52: 8:27; 9:33, 34; 10:17, 32, 46, 52. Only two of these uses have parallels in either Matthew or Luke. Matthew alone has "on the way" (*en tē hodō*) in 20:17b, which roughly, but not precisely, parallels Mark 10:32. Both Matthew (20:30) and Luke (18:35) follow exactly Mark's "beside the way" (*para tēn hodon*) in 10:46c. In the remaining parts of Mark's Gospel, outside 8:27-10:52 and 1:2, 3, the term *hodos* occurs seven times also (2:23, 4:4, 15; 6:8; 8:3; 11:8; 12:14). Of these scattered uses, five have parallels in both Matthew and Luke. A sixth (Mark 8:3) occurs within the scope of Luke's great omission and thus has a parallel only in Matthew. Further, one of Mark's awkward expressions "to make a way" (*hodon poiein*) (Mark 2:23) has no parallel. This contrast in the triple tradition's use of *hodos* inside and outside this section, argues against the view that *hodos* is *always* redactional in Mark as proposed by Johannes Schreiber.[13]

The case for redactional intention in Mark's use of *hodos* in 8:27-10:52, however, is persuasive and rests upon the following considerations:

1. As noted above, almost all of Mark's uses of *hodos* in 8:27-

10:52 have no parallels in Matthew and Luke. This contrasts sharply with the seven occurrences of *hodos* in Mark outside 8:27-10:52, where six have parallels in Matthew and five have parallels in Luke. Hence, the statistical data indicates that *hodos* is a distinctive Markan feature in 8:27-10:52.[14]

2. The occurrences of the term in 8:27-10:52 are strategically placed. Occurring first in 8:27, "on the way" (*en tē hodō*) is thus located in the beginning verse of the section. In the very last verse, 10:52, the same phrase, *en tē hodō* closes the entire section. When one observes that Mark's preceding section, devoted to the themes of *bread* and *understanding* (6:7-8:21), is similarly closed by the section's key term *understanding* (*suniete,* the last word in 8:21),[15] the occurrence of *en tē hodō* at the very end of 10:52 is even more striking. Similarly, in Mark 9:33 and 34 the phrase occurs twice with the effect that the reader should note indeed that the dispute about greatness took place "on the way."

These four texts (8:27; 9:33, 34; 10:52) are Mark's most distinctive uses of the phrase *en tē hodō.* Its crucial use in 10:52 puts the blind man "on the way" following Jesus with now opened eyes. This use appears to function as a contrast to the phrase in 10:46c where the blind man is sitting "beside the way" (*para tēn hodon*), a phrase likely traditional since it reappears in both Matthew and Luke.

In 10:32 the phrase *en tē hodō,* with a parallel occurrence in Matthew, clearly denotes the road leading to Jerusalem. Probably this use was present in the tradition and Mark uses it in accord with his emphasis. In 10:17 *eis hodon* ("into the way") occurs. The rich man is portrayed as running "into the way" of Jesus. He meets Jesus, learns the cost of discipleship, but does not follow "in the way." It appears probable that Mark consciously portrays the 'way' as the intersecting point, not the path, where Jesus and the rich man met and parted. In this view, *eis hodon* is the abortive form of *en tē hodō.* It is the point of inquiry about discipleship, but not the path of following Jesus. Similarly, in 10:46c, *para tēn hodon,* ("alongside the way"), is where the blind sit.

3. Mark consistently uses the imperfect verb to describe the activity which took place *en tē hodō.* In the first three texts (8:27; 9:33, 34), Jesus was *questioning* the disciples, denoted by the verb *epērota.* In the last two texts, (10:32, 52), Mark connects *hodos* with *following* Jesus. In 10:52 the imperfect "was following" (*ēkolouthei*) occurs, and in 10:32 the participle "following" (*akolouthountes*) occurs in the context of other imperfect verbs. In both cases, Matthew uses the simple aorist instead of Mark's imperfect tense.

This quite consistent and distinctive Markan use of the imperfect tense further advances the argument that Mark handles with care that little phrase *en tē hodō*. The action "in the way" begins with *questioning* and ends with *following*. In both cases there is continuing action in past time, a *process* both for Jesus and the disciples.

4. Not only are the *hodos*-phrases strategically located in the structure of the section, but they are also clearly linked to the leading themes of the section. As Norman Perrin notes, in 8:34 the phrase "after me" (*opiso mou*) links the *en tē hodō* of 8:27 with Jesus' teaching on discipleship in 8:34ff.[16] In 9:33, 34 *en tē hodō* provides the link between the passion prediction and the teaching on discipleship. In 10:32 *en tē hodō* provides the introduction for the passion statement. In both 8:27 and 10:46, 52 the phrase is directly related to the christological declarations.

The cumulative weight of this evidence indicates that Mark's use of *en tē hodō* in 8:27-10:52 carries redactional intention. It is with anticipation, therefore, that one looks to the arena of scholarly research on Mark to discover what has already been said on this subject.

III. Scholarly Views of Mark's Use of 'Way' (*Hodos*)

The various scholarly views of Mark's use of *hodos* may be grouped into six different interpretations as follows:

1. *Hodos* is typical Markan scenery, an example of his insignificant *Rahmen*. Like other Markan linking phrases, *hodos* is used to build bridges between previously diverse units of material. This interpretation has been advanced by K. L. Schmidt,[17] Rudolf Bultmann,[18] and Beda Rigaux.[19]

2. Mark employs the notion of 'the way' (*hodos*) to create the transition between Galilee and Jerusalem. *En tē hodō* marks out the *journey* which takes Jesus from Galilee to Jerusalem. This is the position of Vincent Taylor,[20] C. E. B. Cranfield,[21] and Wilhelm Michaelis.[22]

3. Mark's use of *hodos* in 8:27-10:52 not only marks out Jesus' journey to Jerusalem, but it links Mark's teaching on Jesus' passion with Jesus' teaching on discipleship. The 'way' is the way of suffering discipleship. This view, advanced by Ulrich Luz,[23] Eduard Schweizer,[24] Norman Perrin,[25] and Ernest Best,[26] holds that Mark's use of *hodos* is certainly redactional. As Ernest Best puts it in his article devoted to 8:27-10:52:

In our section this sense of motion is brought out by the phrase 'on the way'; it is found at the beginning of the incident of Peter's confession (8:27); it comes at the end of the second prediction of the Passion when the question of greatness arises (9:33); when Jesus makes the third prediction they are 'on the way' going up to Jerusalem (10:32); lastly when Bartimaeus receives his sight it is said that he follows him 'on the way' (10:52). If we go back to the beginning of the Gospel and the only formal quotation of Scripture that Mark makes in the whole Gospel we find it again:
"Behold, I send my messenger before thy face,
who shall prepare thy *way;*
the voice of one crying in the wilderness:
Prepare the *way* of the Lord,
make his paths straight."
Mark's Gospel is the gospel of the Way. It is a way in which Jesus, the Lord, goes and it is a way to which he calls his followers. [27]

4. Adding to these last two interpretations, Konrad Weiss[28] and Karl-Georg Reploh[29] argue that Mark's redactional use of *hodos* is a hermeneutical tool. *Hodos* in 8:27-10:52 contemporizes Jesus' past history so that Mark's readers now hear the call to follow on the way. In this interpretation, *hodos* leads from Jesus' own history to the suffering experience of Christians in Mark's Christian community in the late sixties A.D.

5. A fifth and quite distinctive view is Johannes Schreiber's.[30] Schreiber holds that not only in 8:27—10:52, but throughout the entire Gospel, Mark's use of *hodos* carries redactional intentions. Schreiber argues that Mark's intention is to show that Jesus' entire ministry is a *hodos*-journey climaxing in Jesus' royal enthronement in the temple which Jesus possesses, judges, and promises to rebuild. Schreiber thus contends that for Mark *hodos* holds together both Jesus' cross and exaltation. Jesus' *hodos*-journey to the cross leads to his exaltation.

This writer's response to Schreiber's view is that while it is creative, and at points persuasive, it does not stand the test of exegetical scrutiny as noted above.

6. A sixth most stimulating interpretation of Mark's use of *hodos* in 8:27-10:52 has been recently advanced by Werner Kelber.[31] Kelber observes that Mark associates his redactional use of *hodos* in this section with another prevailing redactional theme, "entrance into the kingdom of God." This phrase is used in 9:47; 10:15, 23, 24, 25, with variant forms in 9:1, 43, 45; 10:14 (note also Mark's distinctive phrase in 11:10, "the kingdom of our father David that is

coming"). Guided by a proposal made years ago by Hans Windisch,[32] Kelber argues that Mark's formula is derived from the Septuagint's Deuteronomic phrase of "entering into the land" (Deut. 1:8, 4:1, 6:18, 16:20). Kelber then concludes that:

... the Markan entrance formula is ultimately derived from a translation of Deuteronomy's entrance tradition into an eschatological key. Modelled after Israel's first entrance, the present journey into the Kingdom constitutes a second entry into the promised land.[33]

With this provocative insight, Kelber suggests that the way (*hodos*) which controls 8:27-10:52 is modeled after the *hodos* of the Old Testament which took the Israelites from the wilderness (or Mt. Sinai, Exod. 23:20) to the promised land. Hence, the first sentence of Mark's Gospel after the title (1:1) is the quotation of Exodus 23:20 via Malachi 3:1 in combination with Isaiah 40:3. In both texts, the key word for Mark is *hodos*. The destiny of both John the Baptist's and Jesus' ministries is the *hodos* to the kingdom of God.

This writer's evaluation of these six interpretations is that all these views, with the exception of Schreiber's position and the one which regards *hodos* as an insignificant reference, contribute to a valid understanding of Mark's redactional intentions. More attention must be given, however, to the last view, for as will now be argued, certain basic structural observations regarding 8:27-10:52 support this interpretation.

IV. The Case for *Hodos* as the Way of Discipleship to the Kingdom of God

The following argument in no way intends to minimize the valid insights which associate *hodos* with teaching on both suffering christology and suffering discipleship. In this writer's opinion, these points stand. What must be added, however, is the setting of these emphases within a larger structural design for this section of Mark's Gospel. Mark 8:27-10:52 models the disciples' journey to the kingdom of God after Israel's experience of moving from the wilderness to the promised land. The evidence for the argument is as follows:

1. As Werner Kelber contends,[34] and Ulrich Luz[35] also recognizes, this section abounds with significant uses of *exerchesthai* ("to go out" or "depart") and *eiserchesthai* ("to come in" or "enter"), imagery derived from Israel's exodus- and entrance-motifs. Kelber considers nineteen uses of *exerchesthai* and eighteen uses of *eiserchesthai* redactional.[36]

2. A second observation supporting this view that Mark's *hodos*-section is modeled after Israel's journey to the promised land is the extent to which the Markan account of the transfiguration utilizes imagery from Exodus 24-32. As Edward C. Hobbs suggests, the story of Jesus exorcizing the demon from the epileptic boy appears to function as a sequel to the transfiguration in the same way as Moses' encounter with idolatrous Israel is the sequel to his experience on the mountain.[37] Both Moses and Jesus descend from the mountain to encounter the unbelief of the people (note Mark's words in 9:19, "O faithless generation" [*O genea apistos*]). J. A. Ziesler has summarized the exodus-symbolism in Mark 9.[38] The parallel themes are the *location on the mountain* (Mark 9:2; Exod. 24:12, 15), and the *six days,* (Mark 9:2; Exod. 24:16); both Jesus and Moses take three persons along up the mountain (Mark 9:2; Exod. 24:1, 9); in both cases a voice comes from the cloud overshadowing the mountain (Mark 9:7; Exod. 24:16); and in both occurs discussion of building tents or a tabernacle (Mark 9:5; Exod. 25:9). To Ziesler's list can be added the glistening countenance of both Jesus and Moses (Mark 9:2, 3; Exod. 34:29-35) and the temporal detail that the voice from the cloud came on the "seventh day" (Mark 9:2, 7; Exod. 24:16).

In addition to these parallels between the transfiguration and the exodus, two further items merit notice. Both the beginning and ending of Exodus 24-32 contain statements concerning Israel's entrance into the land (Exod. 23:23-33; 33:1-3) just as Mark 9:2-9 begins and ends with *hodos*-framework (8:27; 9:33, 34) and entrance-formulas (9:1; 9:43, 45, 47). Second, as Kelber suggests, the statement in Mark 9:1 ("there are some standing here who will not taste death before they see the kingdom of God come with power") carries overtones of the exodus-experience in that only a few members of the present generation will live to see the Promised Land.[39]

3. A third feature which argues for Mark's intended parallelism between *hodos* in 8:27-10:52 and Israel's journey to Canaan is the possible parallelism between Deuteronomy 24 and Mark 10:1-12. In view of the difficulty of how the controversy on divorce and remarriage (10:2-12) fits into Mark's organization in this section, Hobbs' suggestion that Moses' discourse on divorce in Deuteronomy 24 provides Mark with a structural model for 10:2-12 is somewhat convincing. The location of the controversy in Mark 10, "the region of Judea and beyond the Jordan," matches Israel's location for Moses' farewell sermon (Deuteronomy 1:1-5).[40]

Perhaps even Mark's phrase, *ekeithen anastas* (10:1, cf. 7:24) echoes Israel's somewhat aimless but certain movements toward the east side of Jordan and entrance into Canaan (cf. Num. 23).

4. A fourth consideration is that Mark's *en tē hodō* section *ends* with Jesus' arrival at Jericho in much the same way as Israel's journey from the wilderness to Canaan climaxed at Jericho (Joshua 5:10-15). Mark alone among the synoptics has the distinctive phrase in 10:46a, "And he came into Jericho." Both Hobbs[41] and A. M. Farrer[42] have recognized this point.

5. A final observation supporting this interpretation of Mark's redactional intention is the previously noted *hodos*-quotations which Mark uses to begin his Gospel. Mark chooses to introduce his Gospel with two Old Testament quotations elsewhere unassociated in the New Testament. Both quotations use the term *hodos*. The first quotation is a combination of Malachi 3:1 and Exodus 23:20. The second quotation is from Isaiah 40:3.

Much could be said about the tradition-history of these Old Testament texts and especially about the eschatological function of Isaiah 40:3 in Qumran. But these are matters beyond the scope of this paper.[43] What is significant for this study is that these associated *hodos*-quotations confirm the fact that Mark has special interest in the term *hodos*. In both Exodus 23:20 and Isaiah 40:3 'the way' is the way that leads to the promised land. For Mark, the promised land is the kingdom of God.

Beyond these specific textual observations, the case is further strengthened when one observes the crucial function of *hodos* in early Christianity (e.g., the believers were known as "those of The Way"), a matter thoroughly discussed by Eero Repo in his monograph of 1964.[44] Again, these matters are beyond the scope of this study and are themselves substance for other papers.

The cumulative weight of these observations on the parallelism between 8:27-10:52 and the Old Testament exodus- and entrance-events is indeed convincing. Aside from the triple, threefold cycles on discipleship (8:31-38; 9:30-41; and 10:32-45) and the anti-typological features noted above (i.e., the transfiguration followed by the healing of the epileptic boy, 9:1-29; the controversy on divorce, 10:1-12; the pericopae associated with the entrance-formula, 9:42-50 together with 10:13-31; and the entrance into Jericho, 10:46-52) *nothing else* remains in 8:27-10:52. The introductory paragraph (8:27-30) introduces both the *hodos*- and discipleship-motifs. Significantly, the material associated with these exodus- and entrance-motifs comprehends the very pericopae which have always been difficult to incorporate into the section's structural and thematic logic so long as the discipleship-cycles were regarded as the primary structural feature of 8:27-10:52.

A summary of these two major structural components appears below:

Structural Summary of 8:27-10:52

Unit	Anti-typological Material		Discipleship Cycles
1	8:27-30	introductory paragraph	8:27-30
2		for both themes	8:31-38
3	9:1-29		
4			9:30-41
*5	9:43—10:31		
6			10:32-45
7	10:46-52	conclusion to both themes	10:46-52

*The controversy on divorce (10:1-12) is worked into the larger theme of the difficulty of "entering the kingdom of God."

It thus appears that Mark utilizes an alternating pattern of integrating both the anti-typological material and the discipleship-cycles into the overall *hodos*-structure of the section.[45] Both themes fit nicely together within this image of journeying on the way. By carefully integrating these features, Mark presents in this section of his Gospel "The Way of Discipleship (Suffering and Cross) that Leads to the (Promised Land) Kingdom of God."

V. Basic Perspectives from Mark's 'Way' Theology for Christian Thought and Life

Based upon the structural integration of these various themes in Mark 8:27-10:52 several perspectives applicable to Christian thought and life emerge.

First, as Ernest Best has noted, the Christian life is conceived as a pilgrimage. Followers of Jesus are "on the way," moving toward the destiny of the kingdom of God.[46] In contrast to Peter's hope for an imperialistic political vindication of Jesus' messiahship (8:29, 32), Jesus teaches that the pilgrim life does not grasp for power but accepts the cross (8:31, 33, 34); does not seek prestige, but like a child lays no claim to rights or status (9:33-37); and does not bargain for top position, but as a servant gives itself for others (10:35-45). The rich man must divest himself of his possessions in order to become a pilgrim Christian (10:17-22).

Second, the Christian life consists of discipleship, following Jesus' pattern for life, and responding obediently to his teaching. The *way* of 8:27 is linked by the phrase "after me" (in 8:34) to the call to take up the cross and to lose one's own life. To follow Jesus means both copying his example and obeying his commands. We should not dichotomize between imitation and obedience, or between the pattern of Jesus' earthly life and his commands as resurrected Lord.[47] The Jesus of the Gospels calls us to follow after him, to walk the way he leads us.[48] Any view of Christianity that fails to emphasize discipleship as the heart of salvation renders itself inadequate and abortive.[49]

Third, as Acts 3:15; 5:31; Hebrews 2:10; 12:2 indicate, Jesus functions as the Leader or Pioneer, the *Archēgos,* for the Christian. In Hebrews Jesus leads us to salvation through obedience, suffering, and death; in Acts he leads us to life. By making the way of discipleship the walk to the kingdom of God in 8:27-10:52, Mark spatially portrays Jesus as *Archēgos* for those who will follow. Moreover, Mark intensifies this image by making the disciples' servanthood dependent upon, even a copy of, Jesus' servanthood (v. 45 begins with the supportive *gar*).

Fourth and finally, Mark 8:27-10:52 teaches us that Christian victory depends upon Jesus' initiative and our obedience. As in the Old Testament theology of holy war, our task centers in obedience, not in strategizing or fighting.[50] We participate in God's victory through our obedience to Jesus' way and our trust in God's vindication. We hear Jesus' teaching, "With men it is impossible, but not with God; for all things are possible with God" (10:27). The rich man's question." . . . what must I do to inherit eternal life?" and the Pharisees' "Is it lawful for a man to divorce his wife?" reflect the human way of securing kingdom entrance. But Jesus *shows* us the way, *provides* the way, even *gives* us the way to the kingdom; our appropriate response is to follow.

The *way* is first of all *his* way; we share in it through his invitation and our obedient response. As *disciples,* those who follow after, we gain entrance into the kingdom of God.

Notes

[1] The insights of this article are part of a larger perception of Mark's structural organization and pattern. For this, see Willard Swartley, *Mark: The Way For All Nations* (Scottdale, Pa.: Herald Press, 1979). The scholarly development of these insights are in Swartley's doctoral dissertation, "A Study in Markan Structure: The Influence of Israel's Holy History Upon the Structure of the Gospel of Mark," Princeton Theological Seminary, 1973.

[2] *Methodical Bible Study: A New Approach to Hermeneutics* (New York: Ganis and Harris, 1952). Howard T. Kuist's book, *These Words Upon Thy Heart*

(Richmond, Va.: John Knox Press, 1947) reflects a similar approach. Both Traina and Kuist were in turn influenced by Wilbur Webster White, their teacher at the Biblical Seminary in New York. Joseph M. Gettys applies this method to the study of various biblical books in his "How to Study the Bible Series" (John Knox Press). In my judgment, Howard Charles has brought to the classroom the best in this tradition of scholarship.

[3] Among the current trends in structuralism, Erhardt Güttgemann's contributions come closest to Charles's and this paper's method of structural analysis. See Dan O. Via, Jr.'s analysis of Güttgemann's method in *Kerygma and Comedy in the New Testament* (Philadelphia, Pa.: Fortress Press, 1975), pp. 22-27, and especially 76-78; and Güttgemann's own writings: *Offene Fragen zur Formgeschichte des Evangeliums: Eine Methodologische Skizze der Form-und Redaktionsgeschichte* (Münich: Chr. Kaiser Verlag, 1970), now available in English, *Candid Questions Concerning Form Criticism,* translated by William G. Doty from the second 1971 edition (Pittsburgh, Pa.: Pickwick Press, 1978); the journal *Linguistica Biblica,* ed. by Güttgemanns, especially his article, "Linguistischliteraturwissenschaftliche Grundlegung einer Neutestamentlichen Theologie," 13/14 (January 1972), pp. 5-12; and his article, "Theologie als Sprachbezogene Wissenschaft," in *Studia Linguistica Neutestamentica,* ed. by Güttgemanns (Münich: Chr. Kaiser Verlag, 1971), pp. 184-230.

For survey of and introduction to structuralism see Daniel Patte, *What Is Structural Exegesis?* (Philadelphia, Pa.: Fortress Press, 1976); the articles in *Interpretation* (April 1974); and Robert M. Polzin, *Biblical Structuralism: Method and Subjectivity in the Study of Ancient Texts* (Philadelphia, Pa.: Fortress Press, 1977).

The inadequacy of this method, in my judgment, is that it abstracts literature from its historical context, ignores the intention of the author, and therefore confuses "meaning" (what the author intended) with "significance" (how the text now speaks). For discussion of this distinction, see Perry B. Yoder, *Toward Understanding the Bible* (Newton: Faith and Life Press, 1978); further, Norman R. Petersen's *Literary Criticism for New Testament Critics* and Robert Detweiler's *Story, Sign, and Self: Phenomenology and Structuralism as Literary Critical Methods* (Fortress Press and Scholars Press, 1978) point toward helpful correctives to the more purist structuralist approach.

[4] Güttgemanns, *Offene Fragen*, p. 211, and Norman Perrin, "The Literary Gattung, 'Gospel' . . . Some Observations," ET, 82 (1970): 4-7.

[5] Georg Strecker, "The Passion- and Resurrection-Predictions in Mark's Gospel," *Interpretation* 22 (1968): 421-422.

[6] Norman Perrin, "The Creative Use of the Son of Man Traditions by Mark," *Union Seminary Quarterly Review* 23 (1967-68): 357-365.

[7] Philipp Vielhauer, "Erwägungen zur Christologie des Markus-evangeliums," in *Aufsätze zum Neuen Testament;* Theologische Bücherei 31 (Münich: Chr. Kaiser Verlag, 1965), pp. 199-214.

[8] Konrad Weiss, "Ekklesiologie, Tradition, und Geschichte in der Jüngerunterweisung Mark viii: 27-x:52" in *Der historische Jesus und der kerygmatische Christus,* ed. by H. Ristow and K. Matthiae (Berlin: Evangelische Verlagsanstalt, 1960), pp. 413-438.

[9] Quentin Quesnell, *The Mind of St. Mark: Interpretation and Method through the Exegesis of Mark vi.52; Analecta Biblica 38* (Rome: Pontifical Biblical Institute, 1969).

[10] Weiss, *op. cit.,* p. 419.

[11] Quesnell, *op. cit.,* p. 129.

[12] *Ibid.,* pp. 134-136.

[13] Johannes Schreiber, *Theologie des Vertrauens: Eine redaktionsgeschichtliche*

Untersuchung des Markusevangeliums (Hamburg: Furche Verlag, 1967), pp. 190-203.

[14] It might be argued that since, according to the prevailing opinion of synoptic scholarship, Matthew and Luke used Mark and since we can not check Mark against his sources, this observation proves nothing. While this is generally true, accepted method for studying Mark's redactional emphases recognizes the importance of the 'seams'—words, phrases, verses, or even paragraphs—which join together the material common to the synoptic tradition. In this case, 'on the way' occurs at these seams. On method, see Robert H. Stein, "The Proper Methodology for Ascertaining a Markan Redaction History," *Novum Testamentum* 13 (1971): 181-198 and Stein's doctoral dissertation under the same title, Princeton Theological Seminary, 1968. This same methodological point is articulated by Ernest Best in the Preface to his Markan study entitled, *The Temptation and the Passion: The Markan Soteriology* (Cambridge: University Press, 1965), p. 9.

[15] Verses 22-26 of chapter 8 should be regarded as a transitional paragraph between the two sections. The healing of the blind man by a double touch symbolizes the relationship between Peter's confession of Jesus as Messiah (8:27-30) and the unfolding messianic understanding of the disciples pressured by the two bread-feedings (6:30-8:21; N.B. 6:52 and 8:14-21).

[16] "Literary *Gattung*," p. 6.

[17] Karl Ludwig Schmidt, *Der Rahmen der Geschichte Jesu* (Darmstadt: Wissenschaftliche Buchgesellschaft, 1969; reprint of 1919 edition), pp. 216, 230.

[18] Rudolf Bultmann, *The History of the Synoptic Tradition*, E. T. of the 1931 German ed. by John Marsh (New York and Evanston: Harper, 1968, 2d ed.), p. 332.

[19] Beda Rigaux, *The Testimony of St. Mark*, E. T. by Malachy Carroll (Chicago: Franciscan Herald Press, 1966), pp. 8-9.

[20] Vincent Taylor, *The Gospel According to St. Mark: The Greek Text with Introduction, Notes, and Indexes* (London: Macmillan, 1959), pp. 374ff.

[21] C. E. B. Cranfield, *The Gospel According to Saint Mark* (Cambridge: University Press, 1959), pp. 268, 335, 346.

[22] Wilhelm Michaelis, *"hodos,"* Theological Dictionary of the New Testament, 5: 42-96.

[23] Ulrich Luz, "Das Geheimnis und die markinische Christologie," *ZNW* 56 (1965): 24-25.

[24] Eduard Schweizer, *The Good News According to Mark*, E. T. by Donald H. Madvig (Richmond, Va.: John Knox Press, 1970), pp. 216, 221-222, 385.

[25] Perrin, "Literary *Gattung*," p. 6.

[26] Ernest Best, "Discipleship in Mark; Mark viii.22-x.52," *Scottish Journal of Theology* 23 (1970): 323-337.

[27] *Ibid.*, pp. 326-327.

[28] Weiss, *op. cit.*, p. 425.

[29] Karl-Georg Reploh, *Markus—Lehrer der Gemeinde: Eine redaktionsgeschichtliche Studie zu den Jüngerperikopen des Markusevangeliums;* Stuttgarter Biblische Monographien 9 (Stuttgart: Verlag Katholisches Bibelwerk, 1969), pp. 96, 107, 141, 222, 226.

[30] Schreiber, *op. cit.*

[31] Werner H. Kelber, "Kingdom and Parousia in the Gospel of Mark," (Ph.D. dissertation, University of Chicago, 1970).

[32] Hans Windisch, "Die Sprüche vom Eingehen in das Reich Gottes," *ZNW* 27 (1928): 163-192.

[33] Kelber, "Kingdom and Parousia . . .", p. 109. In his book, *The Kingdom in Mark: A New Place and Time* (Philadelphia: Fortress Press, 1974), Kelber reiterates these points (pp. 67-85), but in weakened form since he unfortunately tries to press the material too strongly in the direction of either imminent parousia

expectations or advancing a Galilean Christianity polemic against Jerusalem Christianity.

[34] *Ibid.,* (1970) pp. 108ff., and (1974) p. 68.

[35] Luz, *op. cit.,* p. 15.

[36] Kelber, *The Kingdom in Mark,* p. 68.

[37] Edward C. Hobbs, "The Gospel of Mark and the Exodus" (Ph.D. dissertation, University of Chicago, 1958), pp. 45-46.

[38] J. A. Ziesler,"The Transfiguration Story and the Markan Soteriology," *ET* 81 (1970): 263-268.

[39] Kelber, "Kingdom and Parousia . . .," p. 140.

[40] Hobbs, *op. cit.,* pp. 47-48.

[41] *Ibid.*

[42] Austin M. Farrer, *St. Matthew and St. Mark* (Philadelphia:Westminster Press, 1966, 2d ed.), pp. 193-194.

[43] For discussion of the significance of *hodos* in Qumran, see Vernon S. McCasland, "The Way," *Journal of Biblical Literature* 77 (1958): 222-230.

[44] Eero Repo, *Der "Weg" als Selbstbezeichnung des Urchristentums: Eine traditionsgeschichtliche und semasiologische Untersuchung* (Helsinki: Suomalainen Tudeakatemia, 1964).

[45] In view of this Markan intention, Hans Conzelmann's views on Luke's theological geography need careful reexamination. The following conclusion to his discussion of Luke's journey narrative needs major qualification, if not complete rethinking:

> To sum up, we may say that the extent of the journey report is not determined by the source material employed, but by the work of arrangement carried out by the author. It is he who stamps the 'journey' on the existing material, . . . It is true that he does receive from his sources, particularly from Mark, suggestions for the drawing up of a journey, but in the elaboration and use of the motif for the arrangement of Jesus' life he is quite independent. The journey is therefore a construction, . . . (*The Theology of St. Luke,* trans. by Geoffrey Buswell from the 2nd German ed., 1957 New York: Faber and Faber and Harper and Row, 1960, pp. 72-73).

Conzelmann's redactional study of Luke's journey narrative fails to observe Mark's redactional interest in the journey-way motif of 8:27-10:52.

[46] This emphasis is supported by other Scriptures such as Hebrews 11, especially verses 8-10.

[47] In an article on Ignatius I have described the two main, differing interpretations on this point. One (Michaelis and Rengstorf) excludes 'imitation' as a biblical mandate; the other (Oepke and Larsson) holds imitation as primary to all response. See Willard Swartley, "The Imitatio Christi in the Ignatian Letters" *Vigiliae Christianae* 27 (1973), 86, 87.

[48] For an excellent exposition of the New Testament teaching on Jesus as the pattern for Christian living see chapter 7, "The Disciple and the Way of Jesus" in John H. Yoder, *The Politics of Jesus* (Grand Rapids, Mich.: Eerdmans, 1972), pp. 115-134.

[49] Harold S. Bender's description of *The Anabaptist Vision* (Scottdale, Pa.: Herald Press, 1944) holds that the Anabaptist reformers of the sixteenth century understood Christianity basically as discipleship (*Nachfolge*).

[50] For a treatment of Israel's understanding of holy war as obedience, see Vernard Eller, *King Jesus' Manual of Arms for the 'Armless': War and Peace From Genesis to Revelation* (Nashville and New York: Abingdon, 1973).

8

The Furious Climax in Nazareth (Luke 4:28-30)

Jacob W. Elias

Luke's narrative concerning Jesus' opening ministry in Nazareth (4:16-30) has over the years received the attention of many scholars.[1] However, the significance of the furious climax to these events in Nazareth has not been adequately explored. What is the meaning of the tumultuous conclusion to Jesus' debut in ministry in his hometown? It will be argued here that whatever exact historical event underlies this enigmatic passage its major significance for Luke is symbolic and theological. In his description of Jesus' beginning ministry, Luke includes a proleptic overview of the end of Jesus' earthly career: the mounting hostility against him (4:28), his expulsion from the city (4:29a), his death on the cross (4:29b), and his resurrection and ongoing mission (4:30).

I. Hostility (4:28)

The initial reaction of the audience in Nazareth to Jesus' reading from Isaiah (Luke 4:18, 19) and his announcement of its fulfillment (4:21) was an admiring astonishment or amazement (4:22ab). To be sure, Jesus' true identity was not acknowledged (4:22c), and so Jesus seized the offensive. He predicted the reaction of the people of Nazareth to his future ministry in Capernaum (4:23). Furthermore, he compared his own ministry to that of the prophets who were not acceptable among their own people (4:24), and he cited the examples of Elijah and Elisha, who were commissioned by God to minister to foreigners (4:25-27).

At this point in the narrative the reaction of the synagogue congregation becomes overtly hostile: all were "filled with wrath" (4:28). This dramatic change from admiring astonishment to murderous wrath within the brief time span of a synagogue service has long baffled exegetes and prompted an assortment of explanations. There have been those who have attempted to show that the audience reaction was negative from the beginning.

According to Jeremias, the reason for the anger of the audience is that Jesus ended the Isaiah reading in mid-sentence, thereby emphasizing grace and removing vengeance on the Gentiles from the picture of the future (Luke 4:19; cf. Isa. 61:2).[2] Luke's omission of this judgment motif undoubtedly serves to underscore the fact that the period of Jesus' ministry is characterized by extended grace. It is the time of divine visitation (Luke 19:44; cf. 1:68, 78; 7:16), when the offer of deliverance (release cf. 4:18) is freely extended. However, this message of salvation by itself did not provoke the wrath of the citizens of Nazareth. Luke paints a picture of an initially enthusiastic response (4:22ab). But when Jesus revealed that Nazareth had no monopoly on his miracles (4:23) and that as a prophet, who would not be acceptable among his own people (4:24), he was sent to minister among people elsewhere (4:25-27), the synagogue audience rose up in anger.[3] After announcing that the acceptable year of the Lord was in the process of being fulfilled in his own ministry (4:21), Jesus offended his Nazareth compatriots by indicating that the blessings of the new age were not intended only for them. Not just Nazareth but Capernaum and other cities as well would be the geographical locale of Jesus' ministry. Not just the Jews but the Gentiles as well were to be the recipients of eschatological blessing. In fact, and here lay the major offense, the rejection of Jesus in Nazareth would be followed by his refusal to perform miracles there; the prophet who encountered rejection among his own people would be commissioned by God to reach out to others.[4] Here was a clear repudiation not only of the local patriotism of the Nazareth folk but also of the concept of election held by the Israelite people as a whole.[5] Of course, Jesus' own ministry, even in Luke's Gospel, is almost totally limited to the Jews (although a Samaritan mission has been seen in Luke's central section, Luke 9:52; 17:11), and so the proleptic function of Luke's Nazareth pericope is clearly evident.[6]

What Luke has written concerning Jesus' inaugural ministry in Nazareth is more than an historical account of an actual visit by Jesus to his native place. At that level it is difficult to comprehend the violent rage with which Jesus was greeted on his first public appearance in Nazareth following his baptism. This account of the beginning of Jesus' ministry in Nazareth also clearly foreshadows its outcome in Jerusalem.[7]

Mark's account of Jesus' rejection in his home community also reflects both positive ("and many who heard him were astonished," Mark 6:2) and negative reactions ("and they took offense at him," 6:3) toward Jesus. At the end of Mark's narrative, Jesus marvels at the unbelief of the people (6:6a). Luke has completely rewritten the account, expanding it with other traditions (especially 4:23a and 4:25-27), but he has retained and emphasized the contrasting reactions of the people which are described in Mark 6:2, 3, 6. In 4:22 Luke used the synonym "wondered" in place of Mark's "were astonished" in his description of the astonishment of the audience.[8] Luke also makes a substitution for Mark's brief notice concerning the offense which the people took at Jesus when they pondered the wisdom and mighty works of this young man who had grown up in their midst. (Mark 6:3).[9] In its place Luke has the much more intense reaction of murderous rage, which is occasioned, not by the disparity between Jesus' humble home background and his "wisdom" and "mighty works" as in Mark 6:3, but by the universalism of his message. Luke has, therefore, radically intensified the motif of offense and unbelief which he found in his Markan *Vorlage*, and he has assigned to it a somewhat different basis. Not the identity of Jesus but his message is the primary reason for the anger of his Nazareth kinsmen.

There are no substantial reasons to suggest that Luke has here used any source in addition to Mark. The passive form of the verb "fill" is employed frequently by Luke to describe the process of being filled with the Holy Spirit (Luke 1:15, 41, 67; Acts 2:4; 4:8, 31; 9:17; 13:9). Luke often uses a similar construction to signify the strong emotions and feelings, both positive and negative, which take hold of the characters in his Gospel and in Acts. After the healing of the paralytic the crowd was filled with awe (Luke 5:26, cf. Mark 2:12). When Jesus cured the man with the withered hand, his opponents were filled with fury (Luke 6:11, cf. Mark 3:6). Similarly, after the healing of the lame man at the temple, he writes, "And they were filled with wonder and amazement" (Acts 3:10). On two occasions the Jewish leaders are described as being filled with envy against Peter and the other apostles (Acts 5:17) and against Paul (13:45) because of their popularity with the Jewish masses. Linguistically, the closest parallel to Luke 4:28 is the narrative in Acts 19:23ff. concerning the riot in Ephesus. After the speech by the silversmith Demetrius concerning the threat posed by Paul's polemic against idols, the crowd became enraged (19:28), and the whole city became filled with confusion (19:29).

It is apparent, therefore, that in depicting the opposition of the Nazareth congregation in terms which are much more vivid than Mark's "they took offense" (Mark 6:3), Luke is consistent with his practice elsewhere in Luke-Acts. In Luke 4:28 the reader is reminded again of the setting of this whole episode in the synagogue (cf. 4:16, 20). All who heard what Jesus had just said in the Nazareth synagogue were filled with wrath and ready to take drastic measures against him.[10] Luke's view extends beyond an historical event in Jesus' life to his eventual rejection by his own people. No doubt it also proleptically includes Luke's own time, when Christians were being excluded from synagogues and missionaries were encountering opposition and persecution.

II. Expulsion (4:29a)

Jesus' expulsion from Nazareth is a preview of the crucifixion event with which his earthly career came to an end. That Luke intended in this way to foreshadow the end of Jesus' ministry in this account of its beginning is clearly suggested by the affinity between Luke 4:29a and Luke's version of the parable of the wicked husbandmen (Luke 20:9-19). In Luke's parable the beloved son is cast out of the vineyard and then killed, but in Mark 12:8 the son was killed and then cast out of the vineyard. Luke's parable has been edited to make it correspond more closely to the crucifixion event outside the city of Jerusalem (cf. "out of the city," Luke 4:29). The narrative about Stephen's martyrdom (Acts 7:54-60), which contains themes which are strikingly reminiscent of the crucifixion account (e.g. Acts 7:59, cf. Luke 23:46; Acts 7:60, cf. Luke 23:34), also mentions that Stephen was cast out of the city: "Then they cast him out of the city and stoned him" (Acts 7:58a).

According to Jewish law, executions by stoning were to be carried out "outside the camp" (Lev. 24:13, 14, 23; Num. 15:35, 36). So the proposed execution of Jesus (Luke 4:29) and the actual stoning of Stephen would naturally have been outside of the city.[11] However, Jesus' later crucifixion outside of Jerusalem is clearly being foreshadowed here.[12] In their rage, the Nazareth townsfolk rose to their feet and expelled Jesus from their synagogue and their town. Once again the narrative provides a glimpse into the circumstances of Luke's day. In Luke's writings, "to cast out" is used on occasion to refer to the exclusion of Christians from the synagogues: Luke 6:22 (cf. Matt. 5:11); Acts 13:50.[13]

III. Death (4:29b)

Having expelled Jesus from their synagogue and their city, the angry Nazareth townsfolk led him to the brow of the hill. The words "and they led him" once again anticipate Luke's description of the later events of Jesus' passion. Already in the temptation narrative Luke's introduction to the final temptation (Luke 4:9-12; cf. Matt. 4:5-7) seems to provide a preview of the events in Jerusalem at the end of Jesus' ministry: "and he took him to Jerusalem" (4:9, cf. Matt. 4:5: "Then the devil took him to the holy city"). During the passion week in Jerusalem, Jesus was brought to the high priest ("then they seized him and led him away, bringing him into the high priest's house," Luke 22:54; cf. Mark 14:53: "and they led Jesus to the high priest"), to the Sanhedrin ("and they led him away to their council," Luke 22:66), to Pilate ("[they] brought him before Pilate," Luke 23:1; cf. Mark 15:1), and then finally to the site of the crucifixion ("they led him away," Luke 23:26; cf. Mark 15:20, "and they led him out") where two others were also led away to be crucified with him ("two others also who were criminals were led away to be put to death with him," Luke 23:32; cf. Mark 15:27). Luke repeatedly uses the verb "to lead" to show how Jesus was led from the halls of judgment to the place where he was crucified. When the time had come for the fulfillment of all that had been written concerning him (cf. Luke 18:31; 24:26, 27, 44-46), Jesus allowed himself to be led step-by-step to the place of his death.

Luke states that at Nazareth Jesus was led to the brow of the hill on which their city was built. This topographical detail does not conform well to what is known about ancient or modern Nazareth.[14] A number of attempts have been made to harmonize Luke's description with the topography of Nazareth,[15] but it is probably best not to press the point. Whatever his source for this geographical information might have been,[16] it is fair to say that Luke is more concerned about the symbolic significance of this event than about its historicity. Prevallet suggests that Luke is again thinking ahead to Jerusalem, popularly known as the city seated upon the mountain, where Jesus was taken out to be crucified.[17]

The malicious intent of the Nazareth crowd is specified by the purpose clause, "that they might throw him down headlong." What the devil had tried to persuade Jesus to do voluntarily (Luke 4:9, Matt. 4:6) the people of Nazareth were now about to do to him forcibly.[18] Jesus was to be thrown down the cliff, and then he was to be stoned to death as a false prophet. It is nowhere actually stated that the intention of the Nazareth townsfolk was to stone Jesus.

However, the fact that Jesus, like Stephen in Acts 7:58, was forcibly expelled from the city (cf. Lev. 24:14, 23; Num. 15:35, 36) and brought to the edge of a cliff suggests that Luke was here also picturing an attempt to stone Jesus.[19] In Israel the law prescribed death by stoning for false prophets (Deut. 13:1-11). Jesus had cited Isaiah 61:1, 2; 58:6 to depict his own ministry in prophetic terms (Luke 4:18, 19). To describe his ministry further he had quoted the proverb about the unacceptable prophet (4:24) and used illustrations from the lives of the prophets Elijah and Elisha (4:25-27). Now he was about to be stoned to death as a prophet whose testimony was not accepted as the truth.

IV. Resurrection and Ongoing Mission

In John 8:59 it is reported that the Jewish authorities took up stones to throw at Jesus, but he hid and was able to escape from the temple. At this point a number of manuscripts[20] include some supplementary material from Luke 4:30 to help explain Jesus' miraculous deliverance. It is interesting to note that at least in the opinion of some ancient copyists there was a definite parallel between John 8:59 and Luke 4:29-30. A threat to Jesus' life is followed by a mysterious escape.[21]

Luke's conclusion to his account of Jesus' rejection in Nazareth is striking in its brevity. Jesus' expulsion from the city by the incensed crowd and the ensuing attempt on Jesus' life are narrated in some detail (Luke 4:28, 29), but the outcome of this confrontation is depicted with a minimum of words in a majestic and somewhat enigmatic statement: "But passing through the midst of them he went away" (4:30).

As the visit of Jesus in his hometown moves rapidly toward a furious climax with the seemingly inevitable stoning of Jesus at the hands of the angry mob, the scene suddenly changes, and Jesus emerges the victor. No explanation is given by Luke for this dramatic reversal in the course of events. However, a number of commentators have made their suggestions. Godet and Farrar insist that this was not a miracle; the majesty and dignity of Jesus overawed the people so that he passed unharmed through their midst.[22] Keck suggests that Jesus apparently just took advantage of the confusion, thereby managing to slip away from his would-be executioners.[23] Achtemeier simply notes that whatever the situation, Jesus remains in complete control.[24] Other scholars, however, regard this as a miracle of deliverance. As Plummer puts it: "They had asked for a miracle, and this was the miracle granted to them."[25] Some have detected an echo of the theme of divine protection which is developed in the temptation narrative. In Luke 4:10, 11 (Matt. 4:6) the devil quotes Psalm 91:11, 12 as a guarantee of God's protection. On that occasion Jesus had resisted the devil's invitation to throw himself down (Luke 4:12), but now, when he was on the verge of being thrown down to his death (4:29), Jesus was given this promised protection.[26] It has also often been pointed out that a motif which is typical for John's Gospel appears to be underlying Luke 4:30. At this point in his ministry, Jesus is still unassailable because "his hour has not yet come" (cf. John 7:30, 44; 8:20). Luke nowhere uses these words but in his Gospel there is a similar air of inevitability about the upcoming events in Jerusalem at the conclusion of a period of ministry: Luke 9:51; 13:31-33.[27]

However, the main message of Luke 4:30 cannot be unlocked by reconstructing the mysterious details of this event in Jesus' life. Luke's primary concern here is not biographical. Jesus' victorious emergence from the clutches of the furious people of Nazareth has symbolic value for Luke, both for his account of Jesus' career and for his story of the spread of the Christian church. An examination of the vocabulary of 4:30 within the context of the rest of Luke-Acts helps to bring out its symbolic significance for Luke. Two verbs of movement are used in this brief concluding statement: "go through" and "go." Both of these verbs are used repeatedly in Luke-Acts to describe the progressive forward movement of the ministry of Jesus and the Christian mission. Following the cleansing of the leper in Luke 5:12-14 Luke tells about the spread of the news concerning Jesus: "so much the more the report went abroad concerning him" (5:15; cf. Mark 1:45). Another distinctively Lukan usage of the verb "go through" is found in Luke's account of the preaching and healing ministry of the twelve: "And they departed and went through the villages, preaching the gospel and healing everywhere" (9:6; cf. Mark 6:12, 13; Matt. 10:14). The most extensive parallel to Luke 4:30 is the redactional introduction to the story of the cleansing of ten lepers which is found in Luke's travel narrative: "On the way to Jerusalem he was passing along between Samaria and Galilee" (17:11). One more occurrence of this verb in Luke's Gospel can be noted: "He entered Jericho and was passing through" (19:1). In Acts there are also numerous occasions in which the word "go through" is used. Peter, speaking in the house of Cornelius, referred to Jesus as one who had gone about doing good and healing those who were oppressed by the devil (Acts 10:38). All the other occurrences of "go through" in Acts refer in one way or another to the travels of the early Christian missionaries: 8:4, 40; 9:32, 38; 11:19; 12:10; 13:6, 14; 14:24; 15:3, 41; 16:6; 17:23; 18:23, 27; 19:1, 21; 20:2, 25. For example, Paul in his farewell address to the Ephesian elders describes his now completed ministry among them in this way: "I have gone about preaching the kingdom" (20:25).

An examination of Luke's use of the verb "go," with which he ends Luke 4:30, is even more instructive. "Go" is sometimes used to describe Jesus' movements in the early chapters of Luke's Gospel: to Jerusalem as a boy (Luke 2:41); to the desert (4:42, cf. Mark 1:35); to the centurion's house (7:6, cf. Matt. 8:7); to Nain (7:11). However, the most significant use is made of "go" in Luke's travel narrative, beginning with the pivotal passage of 9:51: "When the days drew near for him to be received up he set his face to go to Jerusalem." From 9:51, where Jesus sets his face to go to Jerusalem, until 19:28-36, where Jesus actually enters that city, there are numerous notices along the way reminding the reader that progress is being made toward the destination. Most of these travel notices use the word "go."[28] Jesus' messengers went ahead to Samaria (9:52), but the people would not receive Jesus since he was heading toward Jerusalem (9:53), so they went to another village (9:56, 57). In 10:38 Jesus and his disciples are still traveling ("as they went on their way"), as well as in 13:22: "He went on his way through towns and villages." Further notice is given in 13:33 that Jesus is moving steadily and by divine necessity toward Jerusalem, the city where prophets perish: "Nevertheless I must go on my way today and tomorrow and the day following." Attention has already been directed to 17:11, which employs both "go through" and "go." Finally, when Jesus entered Jerusalem "he went on ahead, going up to Jerusalem" (19:28, cf. Mark 11:1); and "as he rode along" (19:36, cf. Mark 11:8) the people spread their garments on the road. In addition to these important progress notices in the travel narrative, there are two places within Luke's passion narrative where the verb "go" is employed in an almost technical sense to describe Jesus' coming death. At table with his disciples Jesus declared: "For the Son of Man goes as it has been determined" (22:22; cf. Mark 14:21); and Peter vowed that he would be loyal to Jesus even unto imprisonment and death: "Lord, I am ready to go with you to prison and to death" (22:33, cf. Mark 14:29). Finally there is the journey motif on the Emmaus Road (24:13). The risen Christ, having walked with the two disciples to their village, appeared to want to continue on his journey ("he appeared to be going further," 24:28), but he stayed to break bread with them.

In Acts the word "go" is used on two occasions to describe the ascension of Jesus (Acts 1:10, 11) and in numerous other places to mark the progress of the gospel from Jerusalem to Rome: 5:20; 8:26, 27, 36; 9:11, 15, 31; 10:20; 12:17; 16:7, 16; 17:14; 18:6; 19:21; 20:1, 22; 21:5; 22:10, 21; 28:26. It is significant that the final scene in Acts shows Paul in Rome freely proclaiming the kingdom of God and teaching about Jesus (28:30, 31).

It is apparent, therefore, that Luke's dramatic conclusion to Jesus' tumultuous visit in Nazareth is highly significant as an overview of the whole of Jesus' career.[29] The redemptive career of Jesus cannot be brought to a halt by the hatred and violence of men. When death seemed inevitable, Jesus, passing through their midst, went on his way. The conjunction of these two verbs which occur so often in Luke's Gospel and in Acts to serve notice concerning the ongoing movement of the mission of Jesus and the early church, highlights the fact that not even the violence of men, which led eventually to the crucifixion of Jesus, can frustrate the forward thrust of the new age. After Nazareth, Jesus went on his way to Capernaum (Luke 4:31) and then to other cities (4:43). He also called disciples who went on their way preaching and healing (9:6). Then, when the time drew near for his "being taken up" (9:51), Jesus consciously and deliberately set his course to go to Jerusalem (9:51, 53; 13:33; 17:11; 19:1, 28), the city where the events foreshadowed in the stoning attempt of 4:28, 29 actually took place. But even the crucifixion of Jesus did not put a stop to "the way of the Lord."[30] After his resurrection Jesus continued on his way (24:13-15, 28), and eventually he was received up into heaven from whence he will someday return: "This Jesus, who was taken up from you into heaven, will come in the same way as you saw him go into heaven" (Acts 1:11).

Jesus' mission, which is so clearly foreshadowed in Luke 4:28-30, took him on a journey among the Jewish people—to Jerusalem, to his death, his resurrection, and, finally, his exaltation to glory. In the meantime, the church, empowered by the same Spirit and facing some of the same violent opposition, also moves on with her proclamation. The promise inherent in Luke 4:30, Jesus' victorious emergence for continued ministry, and finally also in Acts 28:30, 31, Paul's free proclamation of the gospel as a prisoner in Rome, would seem to signify for Luke that the forward thrust of this new period of *Heilsgeschichte* would continue despite even the opposition and the hardness of heart of the Jewish people. In the Christian mission, as in Jesus' ministry, the way of the Lord must go on. Faced by rejection in Nazareth, Jesus went to Capernaum and to other cities, and ultimately to Jerusalem. Similarly, the church, confronted by continuing opposition from the Jewish people, directed her evangelizing thrust toward the Gentiles.[31]

Notes

[1] The present writer's doctoral dissertation, which explores this pericope at the redaction-critical level, contains a review of the literature on this passage: *The Beginning of Jesus' Ministry in the Gospel of Luke: A Redaction-Critical Study of Luke 4:14-30* (Unpublished Th.D. dissertation, Toronto School of Theology, 1978). What follows is based largely on this dissertation. The hypothesis that Mark 6:1-6a is a source for Luke 4:16-30 is argued at length in that context; it will be assumed here.

[2] J. Jeremias, *Jesus' Promise to the Nations* (trans. S. H. Hooke; London, 1958) p. 45.

[3] M. Tolbert, "Die Hauptinteressen des Evangelisten Lukas," in G. Braumann (ed.), *Das Lukas-Evangelium* (Darmstadt, 1974) 340-341, suggests that the Nazareth pericope mirrors a pattern which recurs in Acts (e.g. 14:14-52): (1) The gospel is preached to the Jews; (2) they receive it enthusiastically; (3) the universal implications of the gospel are spelled out from Scripture; (4) they reject it.

[4] Some scholars have even suggested that the word *acceptable* in the prophet saying in Luke 4:24 should be interpreted as "acceptable to God." The implication would then be that a prophet would not be acceptable to God unless he went outside his own country. D. Hill, "The Rejection of Jesus at Nazareth," *Nov. Test.* 13 (1971): 168-170; H. J. B. Combrink, "The Structure and Significance of Luke 4:16-30," *Neotestamentica* 7 (1973):38; J. Sanders, "From Isaiah 61 to Luke 4," in J. Sanders (ed.), *Christianity, Judaism and other Greco-Roman Cults* Part 1 (Leiden, 1975), p. 98.

[5] L. Brun, "Der Besuch Jesu in Nazareth nach Lukas," in *Serta Rudbergiana* (Oslo, 1931), p. 14.

[6] S. G. Wilson, *The Gentiles and the Gentile Mission in Luke-Acts* (Cambridge, 1973), pp. 29-58 (see especially pp. 47-48, 51-53), discusses the Lukan view of Jesus' mission, noting that by and large Luke follows his traditions regarding Jesus' attitude toward the Gentiles (Luke 7:1-10; 10:12, 13-16; 11:29-32, 33; 13:18-21, 28; 20:9-19). But in Luke 24:47, after Jesus' resurrection, the universal mission, which is emphasized by Luke in Acts, comes into clear view.

[7] H. Schürmann, *Das Lukasevangelium* 1 (Freiburg: Herder, 1969):239.

[8] Luke apparently uses these words synonymously. See Luke 9:43.

[9] Luke has avoided the verb "take offense" on other occasions as well. See S. Brown, *Apostasy and Perseverance in the Theology of Luke* (Rome, 1969), pp. 30-31. The relevant texts are: Luke 8:13 (cf. Mark 4:17); Luke 22:31-34 (cf. Mark 14:27, 29).

[10] D. Bosch, *Die Heidenmission in der Zukunftsschau Jesu* (Zurich, 1959) 87, sees the "all" in Luke 4:28 as a proleptic reference to the later experience of the rejection of Jesus by the people as a whole and not just the Jewish leadership. G. Lohfink, *Die Sammlung Israels* (Munich, 1975) 43-46, distinguishes between Luke's traditions, in which the people as a whole are shown to reject Jesus (e.g. 4:25-29), and Luke's redaction, in which the people, but not their leaders, are positive toward Jesus (e.g. 4:16-22). He fails to note the obvious signs of redaction in 4:28.

[11] Note, however, that in Acts 14:19 Paul is stoned and then dragged out of the city where he was left for dead.

[12] This is the opinion of many scholars: e.g. R. H. Lightfoot, *History and Interpretation in the Gospels*. (London, 1935), p. 205; W. E. Bundy, *Jesus and the First Three Gospels* (Cambridge, 1955), p. 70; A. George, "La predication inaugurale de Jesus dans la synagogue de Nazareth, Luke 4:16-30," *Bib, Vie Chret.* 59 (1964):25; E. M. Prevallet, "The Rejection at Nazareth: Luke 4:14-30," *Scripture* 20 (1968):6.

[13] On Luke 6:22 see H. Schürmann, *op. cit.*, pp. 332-333. On the exclusion of Christians from the synagogues: W. Eltester, "Israel im lukanischen Werk und die Nazarethperikope," *BZNW* (Berlin, 1972), pp. 143-145.

[14] C. Kopp, *The Holy Places of the Gospels* (trans. R. Walls; New York: Herder & Herder, 1963), p. 50, describes the topography of Nazareth as follows: "Hills rise up all around like an amphitheatre. On the north side the place is closed in by the Nebi Sa'in, 1,586 feet high. The elevations on east and west are less sharply defined. On the southeast a wadi with its more fertile soil forms a glen. One and one-half miles away, this reaches the steep escarpment above the plain of Jezreel. Winter rains have eroded the rocks and fashioned the gully which drops steeply down into the plain." Also see the discussion by K. L. Schmidt, *Der Rahmen der Geschichte Jesu* (Darmstadt, 1969), pp. 42-43; G. Dalman, *Sacred Sites and Ways*, trans. P. P. Levertoff (London, 1935), pp. 73-74.

[15] E.g. A. Plummer, *A Critical and Exegetical Commentary on the Gospel According to St. Luke*, 4th ed. (Edinburgh, 1901), p. 129.

[16] A number of scholars point to the phrase "their city was built" as an indication of an underlying Semitic source: B. Violet, "Zum rechten Verständnis der Nazareth-Perikope Luke 4:16-30," *ZNW* 37 (1938):260; A. Schlatter, *Das Evangelium des Lukas* 2d ed. (Stuttgart, 1960), p. 225; H. Schürmann, "Zur Traditionsgeschichte der Nazareth-perikope Luke 4:16-30," in *Melanges Bibliques* (Gembloux, 1970), p. 199.

[17] E. M. Prevallet, "The Rejection at Nazareth. . . ," pp. 6, 7.

[18] This "Kontrastmotive" is suggested by H. Schürmann, *Das Lukas-evangelium* 1:240. See also N. Hyldahl, "Die Versuchung auf der Zinne des Tempels," *ST* 15 (1961):121-127.

[19] Among scholars who understand Luke 4:29 as the beginning of an attempt at stoning Jesus are the following: G. Dalman, *Jesus-Joshua*, trans. P. Levertoff (London, 1929), p. 53; J. Schmid, *Das Evangelium nach Lukas*, 4th rev. ed. (Regensburg, 1960), p. 114; G. Voss, *Die Christologie der lukanischen Schriften im Grundzügen* (Paris, 1965), p. 158; H. Schürmann, "Zur Traditionsgeschichte. . . ," p. 199.

[20] Successive correctors of Codex Sinaiticus and later uncial and miniscule manuscripts contain a variety of readings which betray the secondary influence of Luke 4:30. For a convenient summary of the textual history: *The Greek N.T.* (United Bible Societies), John 8:59. Also: B. M. Metzger, *A Textual Commentary on the Greek N.T.* (U.B.S., 1971), p. 227.

[21] A. Guilding, *The Fourth Gospel and Jewish Worship* (Oxford, 1960) 109, explains the insertion of Luke 4:30 after John 8:59 in some manuscripts on the premise that the lectionary readings underlying Luke 4:16-30 coincided with those for John 8 and 9: "Both the Third and the Fourth Gospels seem to have been arranged for liturgical use, and it would be quite natural that a passage from the Gospels designed for public reading in the church at any particular season should be 'embroidered' with part of another Gospel lection designed for the same season, especially if the two passages were seen to be based on the same O.T. lectionary readings."

However, L. Crockett, "Luke 4:16-30 and the Jewish Lectionary Cycle: A Word of Caution," *JJS* 17 (1966):43, correctly points out that in both Luke 4 and John 8 an attempt is made on Jesus' life, and both times he mysteriously escapes. "One does not need to presuppose a lectionary background to understand why a scribe would have associated them."

[22] F. Godet, *A Commentary on the Gospel of St. Luke* (trans. E. W. Shalders & M. D. Cusin; New York, 1887), p. 154; F. W. Farrar, *The Gospel According to St. Luke in Greek* (Cambridge, 1921), p. 153.

[23] L. E. Keck, "Jesus' Entrance upon His Mission, Luke 3:1—4:30," *RevExp* 64 (1967):481.

[24] P. J. Achtemeier, "The Lukan Perspective on the Miracles of Jesus: A Preliminary Sketch," *JBL* 94 (1975):552. He also points to Luke 22:51 (Jesus' healing of the slave's ear on the night of his arrest) as another illustration of Jesus' controlling influence.

[25] A. Plummer, *op. cit.*, p. 130.

Others who have similarly interpreted Luke 4:30 as a miracle include: H. von Baer, *Der Heilige Geist in den Lukasschriften* (Stuttgart, 1926); H. Anderson, "Broadening Horizons. The Rejection at Nazareth of Luke 4:16-30 in light of Recent Critical Trends," *Int.* 18 (1964):271; E. Haenchen, "Historie und Verkündigung bei Markus und Lukas," in G. Braumann (ed.), *Das Lukas-Evangelium* (Darmstadt, 1974), p. 300.

M. H. Miller, *The Character of Miracles in Luke-Acts* (Unpublished dissertation, Graduate Theological Union, 1971), p. 22, detects affinities between Hellenistic escape miracles and Acts 12:7, 10; 16:26 but does not mention Luke 4:30.

[26] Scholars who have highlighted this divine protection motif include: A. R. C. Leaney, *A Commentary on the Gospel According to St. Luke*, 2d ed. (London: Black, 1966), p. 120; H. Schürmann, *Das Lukas-evangelium* 1 (Freiburg: Herder, 1969):240; and E. Samain, "Aucun prophète n'est bien recu dans sa patrie. Luke 4:21-30," *Assemb. Seign.* 35 (1973):69.

[27] Scholars who have recognized this Johannine motif include: J. Schmid, *Das Evangelium nach Lukas* 4th rev. ed. (Regensburg, 1960), p. 114; C. Masson, "Jésus à Nazareth," in *Vers les sources d'eau Vive* (Lausanne, 1961), p. 60; H. Schürmann, *op. cit.*, p. 240.

[28] J. H. Davies, "The Purpose of the Central Section of St. Luke's Gospel," *Stud. Evang.* 2 (Berlin, 1964), p. 166n.1, lists 18 notices regarding the progress of the journey to Jerusalem after Luke 9:51. Those which use other verbs are: 14:25; 18:31, 35; 19:29, 41; 19:1, 45; and 19:11.

[29] This symbolic dimension of Luke 4:30 has been recognized by a number of scholars. Studies relevant in varying ways to the synthesis which follows include the following: G. W. H. Lampe, "The Lucan Portrait of Christ," *NTS* 2 (1955-56):167; I. de la Potterie, "L'onction du Christ," *Nouv. Rev. Theol.* 80 (1958):233; C. Masson, "Jésus à Nazareth," in *Vers les sources d'eau Vive* (Lausanne, 1961), p. 63; A. George, "La pré-dication inaugurale de Jésus dans la synagogue de Nazareth, Luke 4:16-30," *Bib. Vie Chrét.* (1964), p. 25; E. M. Prevallet, *Luke 24:26: A Passover Christology* (Unpublished dissertation, Marquette Univ., 1967), pp. 66-67 *et passim*; E. M. Prevallet, see footnote 12 above; H. Schürmann, *Das Lukasevangelium* 1, pp. 240, 241; W. Eltester, *op. cit.*, pp. 99-100.

[30] On the "way of the Lord" motif in Luke's writings: W. C. Robinson, Jr., *Der Weg des Herrn* (trans. G. & G. Strecker; Hamburg-Bergstadt, 1964).

[31] There has been a vigorous debate between Ulrich Wilckens and David Flusser on this issue. Flusser has correctly, in my judgment, shown that Christian scholars (especially Wilckens) betray a degree of anti-Jewish bias if not anti-Semitism when they interpret Luke's treatment of the reception of the Gospel by the Jews. It is surely correct that we must learn to let Luke speak. If what he says is indeed, in the light of our twenty centuries of history, seen to be anti-Semitic, it must be rejected. The problem is too complex to deal with here, and from the mass of literature which has been pouring out on this subject in the past few years, we must content ourselves

merely with a reference to that important debate and Rendtorff's attempt to referee it (*Evangelische Theologie*, 1974). It is also possible that we add to Luke's text an anti-Jewish bias simply by not qualifying the expression "Jewish people." Perhaps even Luke could be persuaded to use that term in a restricted sense as referring to the contemporaries of Jesus and Paul. (This footnote, in its entirety, is supplied by the editor.)

9

The Novel Element in the Love Commandment of Jesus

William Klassen

Introduction

". . . the originality of Jesus lies in his whole personality, in the peculiar energy of his experience of the living God. It is not his concepts that are original, but his power; not his formulae, but his confessions; not his dogmas, but his faith; not his system, but his personality. The originality of Jesus lies in the comprehensive uniqueness of his inner life; the new, the epoch-making thing is himself."[1]

In those words, Adolf Deissmann expressed an influential idea which has shaped the question for many New Testament scholars. They follow Irenaeus in his reply to the Marcionite query: "What new thing did Jesus bring?" with the words: "He brought all that was new, in bringing himself."[2]

It is evident from these words that early in the history of the Christian church the element of novelty in the teachings of Jesus was frequently discussed. Justin Martyr singles out the love commandment, specifically the teaching of love for the enemy, as the new element which Jesus had brought to the world.[3]

In recent times, one New Testament scholar not noted for finding genuine words of Jesus, R. Bultmann, has stated that here, if anywhere, we can find what is characteristic of the preaching of Jesus.[4] Following this lead, numerous New Testament scholars have turned their attention again to the element of novelty in the love commandment of Jesus.[5]

Working in the first century, the writer of the Gospel of John, one of the earliest Christian theologians, already saw in Jesus' command to love one another "the new command" (John 13:34). At least the Johannine circle of churches saw this "new commandment" as the distinctive characteristic of their life together (1 John 2:8-11).

Our interest in the novelty of the Christian love command has to do with more than isolating the distinctiveness of Christianity through a history-of-religions approach. It is also an attempt to get to the heart of the matter, to separate essentials from nonessentials, and to differentiate true from false in the definition of what it means to follow Christ the Lord. The emphasis upon the uniqueness of the love commandment appears quite legitimately then, most often among the apologists of the second century and those who were trying to validate Christianity as a religious movement in its own right.[6] This means that love of enemies demanded and held a prominent place in the proclamation and instruction of the church in the early centuries.[7]

The renewal of interest in this topic, as seen by the attention given to it by New Testament scholars, emerges from several directions, each important in its own right. There is the continuing concern with what we may call the "essence" of Christianity which is seen in Adolf Harnack's book, *What Is Christianity?* (1900).[8] There is the application of criteria for sorting out genuine sayings of Jesus which has brought scholars back repeatedly to this saying of Jesus. There is furthermore, however, the attempt to fit this concept of love into the liberation theology of the twentieth century. Was Jesus a revolutionist? If so, in what way? Vigorous attempts have been made to deal with the teaching of Jesus with respect to liberation theology. The figure that attracts and confounds us all in this respect is Dietrich Bonhoeffer. Although neglected by all technical studies of discipleship in recent years, Bonhoeffer is the one who has captured the popular theological mind.

Christian theologians have had to wrestle with the distance that lies between the early Dietrich Bonhoeffer and the later. In his earliest writing on the Sermon on the Mount Bonhoeffer said: "The right way to requite evil, . . . is not to resist it." He went on to say, "The only way to overcome evil is to let it run itself to a standstill because it does not find the resistance it is looking for. Resistance merely creates further evil and adds fuel to the flames. But when evil meets no opposition and encounters no obstacle but only patient endurance, its sting is drawn, and at last it meets an opponent which is more than its match. Of course this can only happen when the last ounce of resistance is abandoned, and the renunciation of revenge is complete. Then evil cannot find its mark, it can breed no further evil, and is left barren."[9]

To bar the way to every casuistry Bonhoeffer continues, "There is no deed on earth so outrageous as to justify a different attitude. The worse the evil, the readier must the Christian be to suffer; he must let the evil person fall into Jesus' hands."[10]

Bonhoeffer proceeds to deal with the way out of this dilemma found in the Reformed tradition, that is, a distinction of office and person. He argues convincingly that this distinction is not found in the teachings of Jesus. The only blueprint found in the life of Jesus is that the disciple must follow Jesus to the cross.

This witness of Bonhoeffer in his early days was, to be sure, totally eclipsed in his later life when he felt the strong pull to do something about Hitler. At that time Bonhoeffer decided to enter into a dim and uncharted way. He left behind or expanded his earlier understanding of discipleship. He became a member of a conspiracy to kill Hitler under the guise of alternate service. This, in spite of his profound statements in *The Cost of Discipleship* about Jesus directing his words to the way in which the Christian deals with the evil person, and not with evil in the abstract.[11]

We cannot here analyze the various factors that went into Bonhoeffer's boundary situation. It must only be pointed out that involving himself in the plot to kill Hitler was not something Bonhoeffer did impetuously. It gradually became an obsession after his return to Germany from America. It is woven into the warp and woof of his lifestyle and must always be seen, therefore, as representing the conscious reaction to a situation, a reaction which for Bonhoeffer was fully integrated with his understanding of the will of Christ. Springing out of the agony of a concrete situation, the plot was a product of biblical study, a profound comprehension of western theology, and a desire to do something decisive.

The problem for contemporary theology is whether Bonhoeffer should become a model for liberation theology or whether indeed he deserves the designation "Christian martyr," which the German church for other reasons was reluctant to give him. Did his deed have any organic continuity with the Christ who died for his enemies?

Love for Enemies

The recent literature on the New Testament concept of loving one's enemies finds itself more comfortable with Martin Luther King as its model,[12] than with Dietrich Bonhoeffer. It is obviously impossible to use Bonhoeffer as an illustration of loving your enemies, for no prayer on behalf of his enemies is found among his writings. Clearly he saw Hitler as the enemy, but he found no way ever to apply the teaching of Jesus' love for enemies to his concrete situation. On the face of it, one can only conclude that Bonhoeffer brilliantly described the novel element in the life and teaching of Jesus. Unfortunately, he could not follow Jesus' teaching, and he paid for his unfaithfulness to Jesus with his death.

With Martin Luther King, matters are quite different. He, like Bonhoeffer, was gunned down by his enemies. He too saw the enemy clearly, and throughout his life he consistently affirmed that if a black man could not love his enemies he would eventually destroy himself. It could prove instructive to compare Martin Luther King, and perhaps also Daniel Berrigan, with the New Testament teaching on love for the enemy to ascertain whether in these two instances we may not have a more authentic Christian witness than we have in the case of Bonhoeffer. Authenticity in this case is measured by that which is unique in the teaching of Jesus.

I find particularly moving the "Nameless Ode" written by Daniel Berrigan after Nixon's fall. After cataloguing the horrors of Nixon, he writes,

I . . .
would like to pray for Richard Nixon
unsure of what words
could win him intercession . . .
do not I pray
let the earth swallow
nor Sheol claim
nor seven devils return to possess his house
and the last fate of that man be worse than the first
and may the children
who died
be by death
not twisted in form or spirit
into avenging angels
but retain (in death)
their native sweetness

and lead this one
spared for a space
to a better heart

all of us to a better heart
Amen, Alleluia.[13]

Any attempt to draw parallels between Berrigan and Bonhoeffer's interpretation of Jesus must come to terms with the lines written by Berrigan after he read Bethge's biography of Bonhoeffer. Asking himself whether he and Phil would ever have taken the path of Bonhoeffer he replies, "We would not, by any means." It is not that he condemns Bonhoeffer, it is only that he has learned from Bonhoeffer as from Hitler, Johnson, and Nixon "the limits of equivocal gesture."

"We stand with Bonhoeffer, whose struggle was more protracted, who was faithful unto death.

"We, too, wish to be both Christian and contemporary. And this accounts, paradoxically, for the difference between us and him." He concludes his writing on Bonhoeffer: "I am responsible, not to the warmakers and purveyors of violence, but to the community of peacemaking resistance."[14]

Before such a comparison with contemporary spokesmen and the teaching of Jesus is made, we must, however, look at the aspect of novelty found in the teachings of Jesus himself. We have to deal with two sources: the Jewish tradition in which Jesus found himself totally at home; and the Hellenistic tradition in which he was less at home, but which became immensely important for both Paul and Luke at least as they hammered out the Christian theological stance in the midst of a Hellenistic world (see below, footnote 27).

Perusing those sources leads to the conclusion that the idea "love your enemies" was not original with Jesus. The illustrations Jesus uses in the Gospels are already present in either the Hellenistic or the Jewish traditions. What then is new? The command *form*, the *focus* it receives, and the *consistency* with which Jesus lived out this idea.

Judaism

Because Jesus was a Jew, we must first look at the Jewish tradition. Gerhard Schneider states that the novelty of Jesus' love command has been defended along five different lines.[15]

1. It is alleged that Jesus was the first to *combine* love for God and love of the neighbor.

2. Over against his Jewish contemporaries, Jesus was the first to *reduce* the manifold commandments of God to obey the Torah to one, namely, love God and the neighbor. For Jesus, all other commandments are secondary to this one and the whole law can be fulfilled in one.

3. Jesus is the first to *expand* the definition of the neighbor. He included the concept of enemy in that of the neighbor and also qualitatively goes beyond the generalized concept of love for

humanity found in Stoicism.

4. Jesus views love for the neighbor as active goodwill. It is a positive deed in contrast to the negative formulation found in Leviticus 19:18 and the negative formulation of the golden rule found in Hellenistic Judaism.

5. The novelty of the love command is found in the new motivation which Jesus opens up. He bases his demands on the relation of God to people.

It can be shown that all of these five points have analogies in both Judaism and Hellenism which clearly antedate Jesus. Therefore whatever novelty we find in the teachings of Jesus will have to be found elsewhere than in their formulation. It could very well be found in the various elements he places into a new context. Furthermore we must always allow for the possibility that the element of novelty is found in the way in which Jesus himself consistently practiced that ethical imperative. Such a consistency is missing in the Apostle Paul who did not hesitate to speak curses to his opponents, including the high priest (Acts 23:3). These inconsistencies in Paul are very illuminating, and the fact that Luke did not shrink back from reporting them, in an age when Stoicism ruled, argues for genuineness. They remain in such undisputed epistles as the Galatians (1:8, 9) and the Philippians (3:2, "look out for dogs") and stand as a stark reminder to us that it is much easier to talk about loving one's enemies than actually to do so. Surely the wish expressed in Galatians (5:12) that Paul's enemies castrate themselves runs directly counter to Jesus' teaching. Every attempt to extricate oneself from that contradiction is futile and it would be better if we were to accustom ourselves to treating Paul as human and allow these violations of the love command to stand. Even the suggestion that we must not take Paul too seriously here and recognize it as a joke can only insist that it is a joke in very poor taste, to say the least.[16]

Judaism and Love of Enemies

With respect to Jesus' attitude toward Judaism, it is one of the ironies of current scholarship that, beginning with Rudolf Bultmann and consistently with all of his disciples, it is affirmed that the words *love your enemies* go back to Jesus. This even the most skeptical form critics have affirmed. The reasons for their affirmation, however, are inadequate. It is asserted repeatedly that we know that Jesus spoke those words because it was a teaching so radically different from Judaism that he could not have borrowed it from his teachers. What happens now to this "assured result" of criticism if we can demonstrate, as we surely can, that this teaching was found already in pre-Christian Judaism? Certainly we must speak of "novelty" in a different way.

1. With respect to the first thesis traced by Schneider, it is generally agreed now that those sections of the Testaments of the Twelve Patriarchs which speak of love for God and neighbor together are pre-Christian (Dan. 5:3; Issachar 5:2a, 7:6, and Zebulon 5:1). Likewise in the book of Jubilees, that section known as the Testament of Isaac (36) contains the same combination.

Philo also combines the two and, furthermore, reduces all the commandments to this one chief commandment. Presence in Hellenistic Judaism does not lead necessarily to the conclusion that this was found already in Palestinian Judaism as well. In the debate with the scribe recorded in Mark 12, the scribe commends Jesus for his answer and describes it as being right (v. 32), so we conclude that the combination was known and accepted there as well. In any case no such sharp distinctions can be drawn between Hellenistic and Palestinian Judaism. That thesis is untenable. Jesus was not the *first* to combine love for God with love for the neighbor.

2. The second thesis that Jesus was the first to *reduce* the commandments to one is also wrong. It is found in such Jewish sources as the Letter of Aristeas (207) in which Jewish sages tell the pagan ruler that the best way to carry out his mandate is to fulfill the commandment to love his neighbor. In the book of Jesus ben Sirach the golden rule apparently is used to interpret Leviticus 19:18 (34, 15/Heb.). More striking is the statement by Rabbi Hillel (20 B.C.E.) that this is the main point of the Torah: "Namely, what you don't like, don't do to your neighbor." Everything else is commentary on the law (b Schabbat 31 a). Other rabbis like Akiba and Ben Azzai designate the command to love the neighbor as "the greatest all-inclusive principle in the Torah." Prior to Hillel it is found also in Tobit 4:15; Legend of Ahikar (Arm.B 53); Hebrew form of TNaph (1:6); Philo, and in the proverbs of Pseudo-Menander (39f.).

3. The third principle, loving one's enemy, goes back very far indeed in human history. In the Mediterranean world, to say nothing of Eastern religions,[17] the counsels of wisdom of Assurbanipal already urge:

Do not repay evil to the man with whom you fight.
Rather repay with friendliness the one who does evil to you.
Do justice to your enemy.
Be friendly toward him and if someone does evil to you give him

sustenance.
Do not plot evil things against him.[18]

The same idea would, moreover, have been accessible to Jesus through Proverbs 25:21.

There are many other examples in both Halakic and Haggadic material on the Jewish side. One need think only of the Elisha cycle of stories in which Elisha, having stumbled upon a group of Syrian soldiers, strikes them with temporary blindness, takes them to the king of Israel who is eager to slaughter his enemies, but is told by the prophet to feed them instead. The king then puts on a banquet for the prisoners-of-war at which they recover their sight, and returns them to their homeland. The narrator concludes the narrative by saying that an end thus came to the wars between Israel and Syria (2 Kings 6:15-23).[19]

There are enough other instances in Jewish literature where the model of loving one's enemy is found to make it impossible for us to relegate this to a peripheral position. Running throughout the instructions in Aristeas is the admonition to be generous as God is generous. Benevolence to one's enemies is said to be the best protection from their threats (192-231). The writer explicitly rejects the notion that liberality should be shown only to friends: "I think that we ought to show the same keen spirit of generosity to those who are opposed to us, that by this means we may win them over to the right and to what is advantageous to them (Meisner text). But we must pray to God that this may be accomplished, for he rules the minds of all men" (227).

Most striking perhaps is the evidence contained in the story of Joseph and Asenath. In this seldom cited account, Asenath, the pagan who marries Joseph, the patriarch, is confronted with a situation in which she finds a number of her enemies, who in fact have tried to destroy her, at her mercy. When her bodyguards show themselves eager to massacre her enemies, she urges them not to do that for it is not the right way. The right way rather is to forgive their attempt to murder her and in that way to fulfill God's command. We do not know, of course, how widely this story circulated, but it is significant that it dates from pre-Christian times.[20]

A similar position is expressed in *The Sentences of Pseudo-Phocylides*:
If you gird on a sword, let it not be to murder but to protect.
But may you not need it at all, neither without the law nor justly.
For if you kill an enemy, you stain your hand (32-34).

This writer seems to rule out even the use of the sword in self-defense, and a recent commentator describes it as "a rather exceptional point of view in antiquity" and as having an "undeniably pacifist ring."[21]

The Testament of Moses, written about the time Jesus was beginning his ministry, reflects the position that the sacrifice of the righteous will effect an atonement which armed resistance cannot achieve. Josephus the historian, as a spokesman for Judaism, places that philosophy into the mouth of Agrippa when he urges the Jews to submit themselves to injustices rather than to fight back: "There is nothing to check blows like submission, and the resignation of the wronged victim puts the wrongdoer to confusion" (B. 2, 351).

It could be argued that from such positions it is still a large step to say as Jesus did: "Love your enemies." Granted. At the same time, the step that Jesus took was consistent with the long steps which had already been taken by many Jews in the direction of rejecting the idea of retaliation. The majority had in no case taken that position, and Judaism lacked the leadership of a person or group which was prepared not only to propose such a plan but also to act upon it.

It is also striking that Hillel is credited with the statement, "Belong to the followers of Aaron who love peace and pursue it, who love people and through instruction bring them close to the Torah" (Abot 1, 12). About the turn of the century, Rabbi Eleazar highlighted the importance of loving your neighbor in his statement: "Sins of men against God are atoned for from the day of atonement. Sins of men against their neighbors are not atoned for on the day of atonement until you have come to reconciliation with your neighbor" (Joma 8, 9). Ben Azzai, moreover, is probably the first teacher in the synagogue who affirmed that in ethics the most important thing is that man is made in the image of God and therefore he must act like God did. A similar theme is stated in Ben Sirach (18:13) in the lines "while man seeks to be good to his neighbor, God seeks to do good to all flesh." The same writer argues that it is generosity towards enemies which is the best protection, "better than sturdy shield or weighty spear, it will fight for you against the enemy" (29:15-17). This view is based on his belief that God is as a shepherd who is compassionate towards the members of his flock. He seeks to correct them, to train them, and to instruct them and he leads them like a shepherd (18:8-14).[22]

We conclude, therefore, that with the abundance of material found in Judaism, it is inaccurate and misleading to suggest that Jesus taught that one should love his enemies, in contradiction to Judaism. Not all Jewish sources are unanimous, of course, in this matter, but there is enough evidence to conclude that the teaching of love for enemies was taught by Jesus in complete harmony with his Jewish contemporaries.

The story is told in Jewish writings of a Roman who suffered shipwreck and was washed ashore naked, in Palestine. He hid behind rocks and called to some Jewish pilgrims, "I am a descendant of Esau, your brother. Give me some clothes to cover my nakedness for the sea has stripped me and I have been unable to save anything." They answered, "May your whole people be stripped as well." Then the Roman lifted up his eyes and saw Rabbi Eleazar walking with them and he called, "I see that you are an old man and that you are honored by your people and that you know the respect God's creature deserves. Please help me. . . ." R. Eleazar, who wore seven garments, took one off and gave it to him. He also took him into his house, gave him food and drink and 200 denarii, accompanied him for fourteen Persian miles, and showed him great respect until he had returned him to his home.[23] Although the story is slightly more recent than the time of Jesus, there is no doubt that Judaism prior to the time of Jesus also knew this dimension. Jesus, in any case, *as a Jew* taught that his disciples were to love their enemies, and in doing so was in fundamental harmony with the message about God in the Old Testament.

Those elements of the Jewish heritage on this matter which had not been fully spelled out were given an important impetus by Hellenistic moralists who were deeply influenced by the life and death of Socrates. Isaiah and Socrates, who also refused to hate their enemies or return evil for evil, become the two most important influences on the early church's understanding of Jesus.

When Schneider lists two additional elements of novelty in the teaching of Jesus—a new specificity provided for what it means to love the enemy, and a new motivation—we can only say that these could be easily documented as present in Judaism, if space permitted. To some extent that has been done by scholars who are quite prepared to live with the unique elements in Jesus, but would prefer to see those elements as part of the Jewish heritage rather than to attribute it all to the creative genius of Jesus or of the early church.

It is important to recognize that most early definitions of what is new in Jesus are already deeply influenced by the desire, and perhaps the need, to lift Jesus out of his Jewish context and isolate him as someone who had been rejected by Judaism. Jesus, however, seems never to have felt that alienation, except from the small circle of Jewish leaders who together with Pilate were able to put him to death. Obviously, we cannot give credence to those writers who attribute the new element in Jesus to this view of love. For the evidence that either Judaism of the first century or Jesus deviated here from the Old Testament is simply completely missing.

The deepest union of Judaism and Christianity may be formed on this point. For underneath it lies a view of God's love which is fundamental to both religions. There is also a view of what God's people are called upon to be and to do to the stranger, the outsider, and the enemy.

The alternatives confronting Jesus in the first century, while not identical to those of Bonhoeffer or Berrigan or King, were not fundamentally different. The array of Jewish leaders of the first century is impressive. There is Johanan ben Zakkai whose devotion was to the teaching of Torah in the Academy. By refusing to defend Jerusalem and leaving it before it was too late, he was able to play a fundamental role in the preservation and transformation of Judaism after the temple and city lay in ruins. There is Akiba who could not accept a role for bar Kochba other than a messianic one. And there is Eleazar ben Yair whose devotion to zeal was so consuming that it drove him to violent acts of terrorism for the sake of saving the culture and people. He died, presumably at his own hand in A.D. 74, a testimony to the fact that the way of terror always ends in terror. And there is Josephus—general, insurgent, shrewd tactician, historian, self-styled prophet—not a chameleon, but not dependable either. We owe very much to him for his reporting, but somehow one cannot visualize him as a leader of a community. There is also the author of the Testament of Moses.[24] A pacifist martyr prepared to die rather than kill, he was convinced that God's way would triumph in the end.

But Jesus of Nazareth overshadows them all—not because of the novel things he taught, but because of the consistent way in which he related all that he said about God to the way God's actions had been viewed by his contemporaries. He died for his faith in God. The paradigm of Socrates, the just man dying for his beliefs, was reinforced and illuminated by the way in which Jesus of Nazareth also died for his beliefs. This consistency was a great factor in the authority which Jesus' command to his disciples to love their enemies held for them. More than that, Christians believe that God vindicated Jesus by raising him from the dead.

Epilogue

It is too large a task to compare Bonhoeffer and Jesus or Jesus with any figure living in the present. And yet such a contrast is inevitable. For, like those of the first century, we look for models.

We venture the suggestion that it is in the consistency of Martin Luther King's witness to the command 'love your enemies' that the deepest level of his faithfulness to Christ can be found. Daniel Berrigan also, under extreme provocation, never lost sight of this central command of his Lord. Persons like Cesar Chavez and the Austrian peasant Franz Jägerstätter[25] have seen this to be the jugular vein of the corporate life of the church which seeks to be transformed by the presence of Christ. An awareness of the vital energy which flows through this vein could well lead the church today, whether in Latin America, North America, Europe, Asia, or Africa.

There is a great temptation for the church in the Third World to make the same mistakes traditional Christianity has made since the days of Constantine. Our Western theology is replete with examples of a misrepresentation of Christ to further such ends. If, however, Jesus is looked at in the light of Eastern religions and in the light of the nonviolence of Socrates—but above all, if he is seen in the train of Hebrew prophets, like Moses, who were prepared to give up their lives so that their people could live, and who invite their followers to shoulder that same cross—then his originality will be apparent. For one of the new things that Jesus did was to call people to become children of peace (Luke 10:5). Others were gathering sons of light and preparing them for a final battle against the sons of darkness. Still others were gathering the sons of righteousness to fight against the sons of unrighteousness. As far as we know, Jesus was the only one who went about gathering the "children of peace." Of them he made peacemakers. Here a term which for Josephus had the standard designation of one who pacifies a land, namely, a *general*, became important for Jesus. For he saw his disciples as following him in reconciling people with God and with each other. The later church saw this clearly when they used the same term to describe both Jesus as peacemaker (Col. 1:20) and the disciples (Matt. 5:9, Luke 10:6).

Precisely in this term we see something of the genius of Jesus. Peace was on the lips of all Jews of the first century. Many prayed for it, longed for it, and fought for it. The term "child of" was one of the most common ones among the Jews of the first century. And yet, as far as we know, no one apart from Jesus ever coined the phrase:

"Son of Peace."[26] From the various parts of his background and training, Jesus took that which he felt God meant him to use and forged out something which eventually was new. It was new not in the sense that Jesus began by attacking the old. He simply followed God in obedience, and, living as he did in the prophet Isaish, he must have pondered often the meaning of the words:

No need to recall the past,
no need to think about what has been done before.
See, I am doing a new deed,
Even now it comes to light; can you not see it?
Yes, I am making a road in the wilderness,
paths in the wilds (Isa. 43:18-19 JB).

Christians affirm that in Jesus God did something new. A new path was made in the wilderness. Yet that newness is built solidly upon the old, and the relationship between old and new is so intimate that without the old, the new cannot be understood. [27,28]

Notes

[1] Adolf Deissmann, *The Religion of Jesus and the Faith of Paul* (London, 1923), p. 149.

[2] Deissmann, p. 150.

[3] *Apologia* 15:9-10.

[4] *History of the Synoptic Tradition*, p. 105. See Lührmann reference in footnote 5, p. 412 and also H. Braun, *Radikalismus* 2:91, footnote 2.

[5] Gerhard Schneider, "Die Neuheit der christlichen Nächstenliebe," *Trierer Theologische Zeitschrift* 82 (1973):257-275; W. C. van Unnik, "Die Motivierung der Feindesliebe in Luke 6:32-35," *NT* 8 (1966):284-300; H. van Oyen, "Die Ethik Jesu in jüdischer und evangelischer Sicht," *Zev. Ethik* 15 (1971):98-117; Dieter Lührmann. "Liebet eure Feinde," *ZThK* 69 (1972):412-434; Paul Minear, *Commands of Christ*, chap. 4, (Nashville, Tenn.: Abingdon, 1974); A. *Die goldene Regel*, (Göttingen, 1962); Andreas Nissen, *Gott und der Nächste im antiken Judentum* (Tübingen, 1974); Luise Schottroff, "Gewaltverzicht und Feindesliebe in der urchristlichen Jesustradition," in *Jesus Christus in Historie und Theologie, Festschrift für Hans Conzelmann* (Tübingen, 1975), pp. 197-221. I mention those I consider of superior quality.

[6] The most frequently quoted saying of Jesus in the second century was the "love your enemies" saying. See especially Helmut Koester, *Synoptische Ueberlieferung bei den apostolischen Vätern*, (Berlin, 1957), p. 44.

[7] van Unnik, *op. cit.*, p. 285.

[8] The German title of which was *Das Wesen des Christentums.*

[9] *The Cost of Discipleship*, 6th ed. (London: SCM Press, 1959), p. 127.

[10] *Ibid.*, p. 128. I am aware of Bonhoeffer's statement "Today I see clearly the dangers of this book, nevertheless I stand by it then as now." (E. Bethge, *D. Bonhoeffer*, p. 527) written some ten years after he wrote *Discipleship*. Nevertheless, I cannot believe that he was unaware of the disparity between what he wrote and what he did. I therefore regard this as a typical ploy on the part of someone who *had* changed his mind but was not prepared to say so. To change one's mind was not yet fashionable.

[11] *Ibid.*, pp. 131ff.
[12] See Luise Schottroff above, footnote 5.
[13] Unpublished. Used with the author's permission.
[14] D. Berrigan, *America Is Hard to Find* (New York: Doubleday, 1972), "The Passion of D. Bonhoeffer," pp. 39-49.
[15] *Op. cit.*
[16] It could also refer to an exclusion from the people, for Deuteronomy 23:1 states that anyone who is castrated cannot be a part of the people of God.
[17] See the older work by Hans Haas, *Idee und Ideal der Feindesliebe in der ausserchristlichen Welt, ein religionsgeschichtlicher Forschungsbericht* (Leipzig, 1927) and more recently Roy Amore, *Two Masters, One Message: The Lives and Teachings of Gautama and Jesus* (Nashville, Tenn.: Abingdon, 1978).
[18] Cf. W. G. Lambert, *Babylonian Wisdom Literature* (Oxford Press, 1960) pp. 101, 11. 38-48; p. 103, 11. 61-65, and also *ANET*, 422A; 426B.
[19] I suggest a connection here between the Jewish wisdom tradition which speaks of feeding the hungry enemy (Proverbs 25) and the earliest prophetic tradition. This connection has not been explored as far as I can tell, although a beginning has been made with Amos (Hans-Juergen Hermisson, *Studien zur Israelitischen Spruchweisheit*, 1968). It is fascinating that this idea of feeding the hungry enemy appears in Paul, but not in Jesus. Jesus does, however, eat with the enemy/sinner.
[20] Most interest in this book has focused on the question of the sacrament in it. The text I have followed is that of Philonenko. The work of Traugott C. Holtz and C. Burchard is important for our understanding of the work, but I do not follow them in their analysis of Christian interpolations. (For details I refer to my forthcoming book on *Love Your Enemies in the Ancient World*.)
[21] P. van der Horst, *The Sentences of Pseudo-Phocylides* (Leiden, 1978), p. 136, and also his article "Pseudo-Phocylides and the New Testament" in *ZNW* 69(1978):187-202.
[22] *JB*. The editors add a footnote: "God's all-embracing mercy in its instructive aspect, emphasized here (v. 13c, d), appears for the first time in the O.T. at this point" (p. 1059).
[23] *Eccl R*. 2, 1 & 1(28c). See also *Jom tob* 32b (*Rab*, bA1); *Ab*. 1, 15. Cited and commented on by Nissen, *op. cit.*, pp. 75-76.
[24] J. J. Collins, "The Date and Provenance of the Testament of Moses," in *Studies in the Testament of Moses*, G. W. Nicklesburg, ed. (*SBL*, 1973), pp. 15-39.
[25] Gordon Zahn, *In Solitary Witness* (Boston: Beacon Press, 1964).
[26] The absence of all parallels here in Greek and Jewish sources has caused a curtain of silence to be dropped upon this formula. Is it because scholars can detect parallels but are not equipped to deal with the unique phenomenon? Originality often consists of unique combinations. In Schweizer's lengthy article on "Son" in the Kittel-Friedrich *TWNT* there is missing any discussion of this formula as well as in Foerster's article on "peace." The only major exception to this neglect seems to be Paul Hoffmann, *Studien zur Theologie der Logienquelle* (Münster, 1972), pp. 309ff. Morton Smith comments in *Palestinian Parties and Politics that Shaped the Old Testament* (New York: Columbia University Press, 1971), page 64: "In the 260 years from Alexander's death to the conquest of Jerusalem by the Roman general Pompey, there were at least 200 campaigns fought in or across Palestine." This illustrates the longing for peace in the first century.
[27] The way in which the "new" is conceived by the Early Church is ably described by Roy Harrisville in his monograph, *The Concept of Newness in the New Testament* (Minneapolis, 1960). He finds that the discussions of the difference between *kainos* and *neos*, the two words used to designate "new" in the New Testament writings have often missed the point. He concludes that Jesus reveals the eschatologically new world within a framework of time, and that historical

occasions take on the character of the new. Thus it is the penetration of the historical by the eschatological which constitutes the newness, gives to the eschatological its character as historical event, and invests Jesus' place in history with its uniqueness. The new commandment would then be seen as new not temporally, but "qualitatively new as given by Jesus, and thus new in reference to the historical process" (pp. 92-93). Although unaware of Harrisville's work, and still tied in part to an outmoded distinction between *neos* and *kainos*, a recent essay by Johann-Friedrich Konrad, "Das Neue an Jesus. Eine grundsätzliche Erwägung," has come to similar conclusions (Hans H. Henrix and M. Stohr, *Exodus und Kreuz im ökumenischen Dialog zwischen Juden und Christen* (Aachen: Einhard-Verlag, 1978), pp. 154-165.

[28] Space does not permit us to explore the Hellenistic sources in this article. A modest beginning has been made by the present writer, specifically with two contemporaries of Paul, Musonius, and Epictetus in the article "Humanitas as seen by Epictetus and Musonius," in *Studi Storico Religiosi* 1 (Rome, 1977):63-82. Fortunately the incisive article which Luise Schottroff did for the Conzelmann Festschrift in 1975 (footnote 5) has now appeared in English in the volume published by Fortress Press, *Essays on the Love Commandment*, essays edited by Reginald Fuller (Philadelphia: Fortress Press, 1979). It has a wealth of documentation from Hellenistic sources. The major weakness of John Piper's *Love Your Enemies* (Cambridge University Press, 1979) is that he does not explore in any detail the antecedents to the "love your enemies" command, and also he avoids a direct confrontation with the centrality of this command for the early church's understanding of itself. He does provide the first detailed book-length treatment of this theme in the English language—a remarkable fact demonstrating how easy it is for biblical scholars to overlook what for the early church was the central point in the ethics of Jesus!

10
The Apostle's Apology Revisited

John H. Yoder

Introduction

The most striking thing I learned from the critical responses to my *Politics of Jesus*[1] has been the relatively low importance which the critics, even when they were Scripture scholars, gave to basic questions of textual interpretation. The book was presented as an exercise in reading the text of the New Testament with certain questions in mind. Those who disagreed with the book's conclusions, however, very seldom found it fitting or necessary to differ on the grounds that the text of the New Testament had not been read correctly. The differences were stated in a variety of ways but very seldom on the basis of the text.

Critics find it easy to disregard direct textual interpretation, especially when the reading of the text calls into question one or another of the deeply believed axioms of Western Protestant culture. The ability to perceive that what the Bible says is different from what we have always assumed it meant is very difficult to acquire and accept.

It is not simple for an author to deal with this kind of critical response. For it rejects what had been argued without dealing with the scriptural basis on which the argument rests. One can argue with the nonbiblical assumptions which the critic holds and which have kept him from reading the text straightforwardly without being conscious that they are nonbiblical. But to lift up and argue with the unavowed philosophy of one's own culture is difficult.

The other path, which requires more patience, is simply to go back again to the text, to read it still more modestly; with still less confidence that we already know all that it says; with still more attention to historical context and literary coherence; with still more concern to understand, from the inside, the mind of the writer(s); with still more trust that "the Lord has yet more truth to break forth from his Holy Word."

John Robinson, the Puritan pastor who first said the above words within a farewell sermon to the Mayflower "pilgrims" as they left Plymouth, may have had in mind the creation of a theocracy in New England. Congregationalists who have often quoted this text in recent generations may have read into the same words a too modern openness to declare "ancient goods uncouth" and to ride with the currents of modernity. Nonetheless the confession taken alone is the quintessence of the "biblicism" of the radical reformation. Scripture spoke in our past to Waldo and Wycliff, to Luther and Marpeck, to Edwards and Campbell, to Spurgeon and Rauschenbusch—to their present needs and mission, which are now our inspiring past. In like manner, in our present it can be Scripture itself which by the Holy Spirit can say something more than to repeat into a world for which they were not given the witness of those predecessors. What is wrong with fundamentalism is not that it holds too tightly to the text of Scripture (although that is what it thinks it does). It is rather that it canonizes some postbiblical, usually post-Reformation formulation, equating it so nearly with the meaning of Scripture that the claim is tacitly made that the hermeneutic task is done.

I could argue that the hermeneutic task is never done, by appealing to the New Testament teaching about the continuing presence and guidance of the Holy Spirit. I could argue that the hermeneutic task is never done by pointing out that our world puts to us questions which have never been faced before in the same shape. But for the present essay I propose to make the point by reading one chapter carefully. I propose to show it by expositing the simple fact that questions of language, vocabulary, syntax, and grammar are quite evident in 2 Corinthians 5 which are not dealt with directly by the major commentaries, and which, when taken seriously, undercut the cherished interpretations of the past. I cherish these past interpretations as much as my critics do: but that respect for the past and even the ability, personally, to find the formulations of the witness of the past inspiring, or even satisfying, is not a goal of the Scripture scholar.

Resources for Reading the Text

If we wish to reread critically a text with a very familiar meaning, so that it can say something new, there are several kinds of resources which can help reopen our eyes for a fresh reading. Sometimes there may be simple matters of grammar and lexicography. Such are present in 2 Corinthians 5, especially (as we shall see later) in the key text which is usually translated "he is a new creature," where both the definition of the individual word "creature" and the construction of the sentence with "he is. . ," as usually rendered, are counter to standard grammatical rules.

A second resource for refreshing one's reading is the broader question of literary coherence: how does one sentence lead into another? This test cannot *always* apply. Some kinds of texts do not claim to be literally coherent: this may be the case for collections of proverbs, and it may be the case if at some point the text we have is the result of editing which combined several earlier documents. Some people claim this is the case for 2 Corinthians, but even that kind of hypothesis would not cut every small text into small pieces. Thus it is fitting to ask this more holistic question of literary coherence. When we do this, we observe that the sequence of the first few sentences of the chapter does not yield an evident thought process if we presuppose that all of the sentences are declarative rather than interrogative. If, however, we take some of the sentences not as declarations but as questions, the thought process becomes evident.

A third kind of resource for refreshing one's reading is to increase one's empathy with the background within which the author was writing and with the overall purposes of the document. For centuries the writings of the Apostle Paul were read as if they were meant to be sources of finely coined phrases ready to be integrated into a system of theology. Then more recently, they were read by many as a series of statements about the self-understanding of the believer as he sees his life in the light of faith. Without denying the element of truth in each of those past (post-Renaissance) assumptions, scholars in recent generations have seen how much more helpful it is to begin at the beginning with the fact that a missionary who had planted some churches, and was concerned as well for the faithfulness of others which he had not planted (as at Rome), is writing letters to those churches because of his concern for how they deal with specific problems of being the church in a pagan world. He cares especially about the problems of being a missionary church which proclaims and incarnates a Jewish message in a Gentile world.[2]

This fact about the ministry of the Apostle Paul was never denied in the past, but it was thought to have little to do with the interpretation of the particular concerns of particular paragraphs and propositions. To be more aware of the pervasive presence of the Jew/Gentile agenda brings to life many sections of the Pauline writings which otherwise seemed much less clear. We possibly may expect to be aided in our access to the meaning of our passage by being reminded that the particular criticisms against which the apostle is defending himself in chapter five as well as in much of the second letter to the Corinthians have to do with the fact that he is committed to bringing into being communities where Jew and Gentile alike confess the faith of Abraham. There were other Christians (including among them Hellenistic Jews) who wanted a more open attitude toward Gentile wisdom and culture. Such an attitude, they argued, should not go to the trouble of dragging along, as a part of the mission method and message, Jewish ideas, Jewish prayers, the Jewish Scriptures, and fellowship with the Jewish church in Syria and Jerusalem. There were other fellow believers (including among them very possibly some Gentiles whose conversion to Jewish practice was ritualistic)[3] who insisted that what the Gentiles had to enter into was the totality of a pre-Messianic and less than missionary Jewish lifestyle. Under attack from both sides, the Paul whom we are reading in 2 Corinthians, the Paul of Acts, and the Paul of Ephesians, has to be understood as doing a third and unheard-of thing: creating a community which is *at the same time* aggressively open to the Gentile world and firmly committed to Abraham and to his children as the only way to know the God of Abraham. It is the defense of this missionary particularism[4] that makes sense of all of the ministry of Paul, and specifically of his self-defense in our text.

Detailed Specimens

The necessary rereading which this approach calls for would of course demand detail which this essay cannot provide. I must limit myself to two specimens, neither of them conclusive, yet each of them quite significant standing alone, and, when combined, certainly sufficient to sustain the thesis that a coherent picture of the thrust of the chapter fitting both of these observations could be developed which would make better sense of the text than the traditional readings.

Is it "Terror" Which Motivates Mission?

The Bible translation produced by James Moffatt, first copyrighted in 1922, with final revisions in 1934, was a pioneer in the realm of new Bible versions. Well before the paraphrase approach of

Phillips and the "dynamic equivalent" theories of translators in the 1970s, Moffatt abandoned the notion of word-for-word and phrase-for-phrase equivalents, and tried to restate the argument or the narrative of a text in good contemporary English, even if this meant presenting different words in different sequence or changing the parts of speech. He did not, however, mean to be producing a paraphrase by adding new thoughts to what was already in the text.

Moffatt was also innovative in that he went out of his way to be open to alternative interpretations of the texts' actual meanings, rather than giving the traditional interpretations the benefit of the doubt. His translation of 2 Corinthians 5:11-15 is a good example of this kind of innovation. Moffatt presents nothing which is not rooted in the literal Greek text. Yet he gives freedom to more imagination in the varied possible literal meanings of that text. Specifically, in this context, the innovation comes from his taking more seriously a fact which all scholars recognize, namely that the received Greek text does not provide the pointers to interpretation which for us are the punctuation marks, in this case the question mark or interrogation point (?) and the quotation mark or inverted commas ("). Sometimes nothing in the Greek text indicates where one of these belongs. This does not mean that quotations do not happen, or that questions are not written in Greek, but only that the signal for what is to be taken as a quotation or as a question must come from the reader's understanding of the context and the flow of the words, since there is no visible mark in the manuscript text. Sometimes an interrogative particle (e.g. "how") or a pronoun ("who") signals a question. Sometimes doubt is signaled by the particle *mē*, but not always. Thus it is always hypothetically possible to consider *any* particular segment of a Greek text as being a quotation rather than the author's own words or as being a question rather than an affirmation. Moffatt makes use of this possibility in a way which clarified considerably the thought pattern of this text. He places quotation marks in significant places to show what others were saying, accusations to which he was responding thus:

Verses 11-15: The Constraint of the Love of Christ

If I 'appeal to the interests of men,' then, it is with the fear of the Lord before my mind. What I am is plain to God without disguise, plain also, I trust, to your own conscience. This is not 'recommending myself to you again'; it is giving you an incentive to be proud of me, which you can use against men who are proud of externals instead of the inward reality. 'I am beside myself,' am

I? Well, that is between myself and God. I am 'sane,' am I? Well, that is in your interests; for I am controlled by the love of Christ, convinced that as One has died for all, then all have died, and that he died for all in order to have the living live no longer for themselves but for him who died and rose for them.

The King James language says for the first of these sections, "knowing the terror of the Lord, we persuade men." In the Authorized Version the affirmations are all simple indicatives, an outright statement either of what Paul himself holds (the "we," of course, means first of all Paul) or of what is true for all Christians or all apostles.

There are two immediate reasons for not assuming that this simple indicative expression is adequate. One is that the word "fear" or "terror" in this position is given a tone which is different from elsewhere. Nowhere else in the New Testament is the phrase "fear of the Lord" translated with the special sense of "terror." It regularly means something much nearer to "reverence" or "respect" than to fright. This is a question not only on the level of word usage but also on that of meaning. It is not said generally in the New Testament that the motivation for mission is the fear of punishment, either for oneself or for the lost men and women to whom one preaches. Fear of hellfire is a motivation of modern Western religion. It is for that reason that this meaning of the text appears to us to be so congenial and therefore so self-evident. This text, interpreted in this way, is, however, the only proof text in the New Testament for the notion that the fear of perdition (either for oneself if one fails to be obedient in evangelizing, or for the hearers in case one does not win them) is the best way to state the missionary motivation. In other words, if it is equally possible to interpret this text in another way, then that entire doctrine, so questionable from the perspective of the rest of the New Testament, and yet so self-evident in Western culture, must be reevaluated.[5] It is a fundamental reason for suspicion, with regard to *any* particular interpretation, if it states a meaning dependent on only that one text, or if we are not free to test it because of the fear that some cherished postbiblical preaching emphasis might have to be tested by the rest of Scripture.

The second clearly verbal question in the first sentence is the use of the word which the King James Version translated "persuade." In modern English, "to persuade" others is generally thought of as a very good thing to do. But the verb *peitho* which it translates is, in the language of Paul and his critics, a term of reproach usually translated "to please." A direct parallel is Galatians 1:10: "Am I now seeking the favor of men or of God? Or am I trying to please men? If I were still pleasing men, I should not be a servant of Christ." It is obvious that, for Paul, to please God is a good thing, but to please oneself or to please men is not. How could Paul, who in Galatians 1 defends himself against his detractors by saying he is not pleasing men, be here defending himself against relatively similar detractors by saying that he *is* pleasing men? On the basis of the general meaning of that verb, a usage in which the standard meaning of *peitho* could be respected is to be preferred to one in which it is given an otherwise rare affirmative meaning as another word for evangelism.

I have referred to two specific terms which make questionable the King James interpretation. We must make one further literary observation about the entire paragraph. In the context of his defending himself against criticisms of his ministry, Paul repeats other accusations which have been leveled against him: that he is recommending himself (v. 12) and that he is insane, ("beside himself," v. 13). Since these next two thought units deal with reproaches addressed to Paul and his defense against them, it would certainly be in order to think of the first unit of the paragraph (v. 11) as also playing back a reproach.

This background should suffice to explain why it would be credible to interpret the passage as a series of three responses to three parallel accusations directed against Paul by the critics of his ministry. The translation I now suggest is like that of Moffatt in substance, but I present it here in a more phrase-by-phrase sequence, so that its literal basis in the text and its parallel to other translations can be more easily checked. I add question marks, as well as quotation marks, to make the dialogical style still clearer.

(11) [Do you say that] I who know what it means to fear the Lord am "pleasing men"? I am fully transparent before God, and I hope also to be transparent before your consciences. (12) I am not 'recommending myself again,' but only giving you a basis for rejoicing on my behalf so that you can answer those who pride themselves on a person's appearance rather than on the heart. (13) Am I [as they say] "crazy"? It is for God's sake. If on the other hand I am in my right mind, this works out for your good (14) for the love of Christ constrains me. . . .

This translation has the advantage of leading us directly into the ensuing text of verse 15, but that is the point where it differs least from the King James interpretation. It also has the advantage of taking the form of three direct responses to three reproaches, roughly identical but different in phrasing, each of them giving Paul the occasion for a different defense. In each case the reproach is addressed not to Paul's message but to his personality style and his sincerity. His first response is that the accusation is not credible because it does not fit with his understanding of the fear of God or his openness to others. The second time he responds by giving an alternative interpretation of what he is doing, when he does adduce arguments which may sound like his "commending himself." The third time he responds rhetorically by saying, "So what? If I am unbalanced it is for the sake of God, who is worth being crazy about."

To "please men" is worthy of reproach not only or primarily because it indicates that the person who tries to please others is not being fully honest, independent, and driven only by the truth. But it further suggests that the way he is trying to appeal to the others is not by serving their best interests or the interest of the truth but appealing to their selfishness or their desire to be flattered. This is why Moffatt uses the phrase, "Appeal to the interests of men."

R. H. Strachan, author of the volume in question in the Moffatt Commentary series, supports this general pattern of interpretation, making an alternative proposal to understand verse 14. The Greek reads more briefly than above: "If I am crazy [that is] for God, if I am sane, [that is] for you."[6] Most translations, like mine above, take "for God" and "for you" as meaning in each case "for the sake of" or "in the interest of." Strachan proposes rather that Paul should be asking who is to pass judgment on the matter. "If I am beside myself, it is to God that I am accountable for that, God should be the judge: if on the other hand I am behaving sanely, that is up to you to deal with, that is something you can judge, I am accountable to you."[7]

This alternative translation does not change the thrust of my general argument here. It still assumes that the accusation of insanity was addressed to Paul and that his response to it was not simply to try to ward it off with counter argumentation but to turn it sideways by going on, "so what if it is the case that I am beside myself. . . ?"

The interpretation of the passage, since Moffatt, has not paid serious attention to this alternative punctuation pattern and the simplification of the meaning which it offers. The French commentator Jean Hering, without indicating any awareness of Moffatt, is one who reads with quotation marks as does Moffatt, without explaining himself.[8]

In the absence of serious attention to the hypothesis stated here, it cannot be considered either as refuted by the fact that it has not been picked up by others, nor as sustained by the absence of negative response to Moffatt. It therefore must remain a worthwhile hypothesis, no more but also no less. We are free to assume it as part of a larger hypothetical synthesis.

Is Conversion Mainly "Inward"?

Our first specimen question exemplifying the difference between our habitual assumptions and the simple meaning of the text in its context had to do more with Paul's self-understanding but less with the content of his message. A more critical specimen of this problematic is the interpretation of verse 17 of this chapter, which is the *locus classicus* for a particular modern Protestant view of conversion. "If any man is in Christ, he is a new creature," the King James Version renders it. The "new creature" is then a new individual human person, made new at some very deep level of what it means to be a human person. This is so profoundly assumed to be the point of the text that it is very difficult for a conservative Protestant reader to let the text speak for itself.

What is then the traditional interpretation of the passage? First of all it is clear that it is a statement about the individual. It is in the singular. It makes a statement about this one person, any person, who is in Christ, who is "a new creature."

Second, it is clear in the prevalent interpretation that this person in himself (or herself) has a new *nature*, is different in the root of what constitutes him as a human organism. Of course this transformed person is in some sense the same person he was before, but the weight of the affirmation is upon the newness which has been given. Not only is the newness located in the "nature" or "essence" of the individual: the "nature" is itself located *within* the person, away from any social or empirical tangibility. The "Living Letters" paraphrase puts it most pointedly; "When someone becomes a Christian he becomes a brand new person inside." The individualizing change goes on: "the old things are gone" becomes "he is not the same any more," and "they have become new" is changed to "A new life is begun."

Third, this event took place some time in the past. It is not clear whether it needs to be conceived as instantaneous or as a process taking some time; but it is definitely a process having happened in the past for any person who is "in Christ." To be in Christ is not a matter of more or less, but of yes and no. Whether conversion is therefore a matter of several minutes or several months, in any case, it is now possible to speak of it as past and achieved. To be "in Christ" and to be a "new creature" is in one sense at least a finished happening.

Fourth, this change in nature involves a *divine work* in the personality of the new creature. This is the significance of the very word *creature*. It points to the divine intervention having created something new. It is not implicit in what relationship this novelty stands to other kinds of causation which make a person what he is (to this question we shall return), but in any case a distinct divine intervention is affirmed. For us to be able to affirm it as solidly as it is usually understood, it must be discernible, not merely be an affirmation of faith with no visible evidence.

It should not be necessary to outline the strength or the attractiveness of this way of conceiving the gospel message. It has definite implications, many of them evidently positive, for the attractiveness of the gospel invitation for those to whom it is addressed, as well as for the appropriateness of the call to a fuller discipleship when this call is addressed to those who have affirmed that they are in Christ. It might further be pointed out (because this is less definitely to be counted as an unequivocal advantage) that this individualistic view is very compatible with modern Western understandings of man.

Questions

Before proceeding to identify the grounds for suggesting that the text in question, and perhaps the entire New Testament, might be making a somewhat different point, let us proceed beyond the self-evident strength of this interpretation to recognizing a few of its handicaps in contemporary thought. For the following reasons I suggest these handicaps before moving to the alternative exegesis:
- a) To make more visible by example the extent to which this thought pattern is predominant and sets the rules of the game for any other discussion;
- b) To suggest some of the unanswered problems we may keep in mind when we come back to read the text anew;
- c) To attempt to loosen up our settled axioms so as to be more able to read the text with open eyes.

Models of the Human

One kind of question which is especially important if the passage is interpreted in the traditional way, but also especially difficult, is how to relate this conception of the transformed believer to the way in which different kinds of discourse, sciences, and theories also try to understand the wholeness of the human being. If we say that a human being is transformed at the root of what makes him what he is, that must certainly relate somehow to the tools of analysis of other people who also claim to be dealing with the roots of what makes a human being what he is. What makes a human person what he or she is in terms of personality is profoundly correlated with the nervous system. Who a person is can be influenced by electric shocks applied to that nervous system, by chemicals, by brain surgery, and other kinds of intervention in the personality which are not mental or spiritual at all in the traditional understanding. Whatever the relationship of the life of the nervous system and the life of the spirit may be, at least there seems to be some kind of serious correlation. For example, there is biochemical physiology, according to which man is made what he is by his DNA, and continues to become and remain what he is by virtue of the electrochemical events in his nerve cells. These are the ways the first creation worked to make humanity human. Does the new creation work this way? Would sufficient sophistication enable us to find how conversion changes a person's DNA or his or her neural electrochemistry?

Another level of the reality of what it means to be a person is that which is dealt with by the various schools of psychology. There are behavior patterns which are learned and can be unlearned. There are complexes and syndromes which are the product of the interaction between the individual needs and appetites on one hand and the family and social environment on the other. Especially, certain major figures in the early life of a child and certain pivotal experiences in development through adolescence are generally understood to have much to do with defining who a person is. Does conversion change syndromes and complexes? If so, does it do so through experiences of learning and unlearning which are themselves subject to psychological interpretation, or does it happen on some other level? Is the new birth a cathartic self-understanding? Does it provide one with a better father image (in God) or ego model (in Jesus) which thereby enables one to cope more adequately? There is also a pedagogical view of the nature of the whole person, which sees him as a learner, acquiring skills and awarenesses. Is conversion a "learning"? Does it fit on a scale of "moral development"?

These questions could be asked with an intention which might be flippant or destructive. That is not my intent. The fact needs simply to be faced that if we do claim in any concrete sense that conversion changes who a person really is, we cannot avoid the encounter with questions of the kind which are asked by the secular disciplines which also deal in their ways with what a person really is. Would we claim that conversion in the heart has no correlate in the biochemistry of the nerves or in the psychodynamics of the personality? Or do we argue a kind of correlation so that conversion could, with adequate tools, be measured by the psychologist or the neurologist?

I ask the question because it is impossible in our time to take the language of conversion seriously without asking it. But by asking it I have pointed out backhandedly that when the classic Protestant understanding of conversion developed in the first place, whether we think in the most precise sense of the most highly developed conversion theories of the revivalists of North America from Edwards to Finney, or whether we go back to the description of the faith which justifies in Luther or the vision of God in the late medieval mystics, none of the people we would be trying to understand would have been saying *then* that conversion is an event in the field of psychodynamics or neurology. So whether we affirm some kind of positive correlation between the several levels, or deny that there is any connection at all and thereby refuse to converse with the modern sciences of man, in either case it raises questions of correlation which were not there before. The gospel promise of transformation talks about the human person as he or she really is; so do these other kinds of analysis. If they are all talking about the same person, then it would seem that we should expect that as they cover the same ground their measurements and descriptions would somehow connect. Do we want our phrasing of the claims and promises of the gospel to be tested by these other disciplines? Or do we rather mean to take the other approach, that of compartmentalization, saying that though we all deal with the same human being, the ways we deal with him are not at all on the same level? There are several classical ways to try to resolve this problem, and all of them seem to have serious logical and practical shortcomings.

If a Christian really believes that there has been physical healing, such as the lengthening of a leg or the removal by miracle of a cancer, it will be a part of the authenticity of that witness to claim that X rays or other medical verification could be appealed to. In a simple similar way, it probably should be assumed that if there is concrete reality to conversion as a change of what the person really is, it could be measured by the scientists. The fact that one does not see many conversionist Christians doing that scientific work does not necessarily prove they would not believe in it, nor that it could not be done. The fact that traditional conversionist preaching and pastoring does go on without driving people into the interdisciplinary encounter does, however, leave the door open for an alternative interpretation, both of Paul and of what has been the really operational validity of the conversion message.

Individual or Social?

A second broad area of difficulty is the relation between this conception of the transformed individual and the social dimensions of the gospel. One of the most clear and sweeping convictions of the mainstream of evangelical preaching is the promise that when an individual is transformed he will live differently in such a way as to transform society in its turn. It is fruitless, it is often argued (or some even argue that it is evil), to attempt to change society in any other way, such as by education or legislation; social change will come when the hearts of individual people are transformed.

Nevertheless, the same evangelical proclamation which promises a transformed society is often able to give very little help in defining how society must be transformed when people are changed. Will people become Democrats or Republicans or socialists, or will they withdraw from politics? Will they want a society that has more free enterprise or less? Will they work for racial integration or for segregation? As a matter of logic, the claim that the transformed person will *automatically* work socially in the right way does not lead us to expect much guidance as to how he should work. No less than the "inward change," this thesis calls for empirical verification. As a matter of record, this kind of evangelical theology has produced both very progressive and very reactionary social strategies. On the basis of both the record and the logic, we can affirm that the transformed person has a different *motivation*, but it certainly is unproven that the transformation carried with it univocal instructions about how society must change, when that transformation had been defined in terms of the individual's constitution, self, or "heart." The purpose of this observation is not to try to resolve the question of the basis or direction of social concern, but simply to record that to locate the saving work of God in the constitution of the person does not tend to throw a very precise light on these questions, even though it promises to.

A third drawback of the emphasis upon the novelty of the new creature is that it may undermine the capacity of the church to speak in Christian education and pastoral care to those who have this event well behind them. The temptation is real to limit later religious experience to a reiteration of the meaning of the born-again experience, and to center Christian service and activity on trying to bring other persons to that same threshold. The promise of a miraculously given new nature in Christ may lead a sensitive believer to despair when he or she discovers how much of the "old man" is still within. At the same time the insensitive and self-satisfied person may insulate him or herself against pastoral admonition and the call to growth in grace by the assurance that the most important event, that which happens back at the beginning of the Christian life, has all been taken care of and now needs only to be maintained.

I do not mean to suggest that these distortions are inevitable results of a strong emphasis on the transformation of a person. They are not even quite as logically necessary as are the other two limitations spoken of above; but that such distortions *can* happen is easily documented from anyone's pastoral or counseling experience.

A fourth shortcoming, at least in contemporary American society, is the temptation to correlate the praise of the novelty of the "new creature" with the modern Western cult of youth, health, and beauty. This modern temptation in aggressive evangelicalism might be spoken of as the "Campus Crusade syndrome"—the expectation that the gospel has a special attraction for, or a special tendency to produce, beauty queens and sports heroes. The correlation of this temptation with this text was dramatized by a denominational church bulletin used in a church I attended. The cover bore the words, "In Christ . . . a new creature." In one corner of the page there was a skidrow face; wrinkled, bleary-eyed, unkempt and unshaven, staring pointlessly into empty blackness; contrasting with him was a healthy young Anglo-Saxon figure, well combed and shaven and dressed, with both feet confidently planted in an athletic pose, his chest swelled out and his eyes gazing at some distant star. Certainly the artist did not mean to promise that an ancient wino can become a young athlete. But the fact that this juxtaposition of images seemed to him to be appropriate to represent newness of life is sufficient documentation that "newness" is likely to be confounded with physiological or psychological image definitions which have little to do with the gospel.

It was, after all, in the same passage that the Apostle Paul had just spoken of having to bear in his body the suffering of Jesus. It was in his same Corinthian correspondence that he spoke of living with a thorn in his flesh, and of the imminent passing away of the "tent" in which he was now living. Whereas much modern evangelicalism calls the individual from brokenness to wholeness, there is another tradition, [Luther, Keswick, going back to Paul, and to Ezekiel and Jeremiah] which calls him from the search for wholeness to the acceptance of brokenness. From this perspective the American glorification of the healthy self appears unevangelical, even demonic.

The converse side of this temptation is the concentration of gospel witness upon the down-and-outer. A middle-class Protestant would feel almost embarrassed about speaking to his middle-class neighbor about Christian faith, but can feel it somehow fitting to drive fifty miles to a rescue mission where there are people who, he can convince himself, are in need of the gospel. This is simply the flip side of the Norman Vincent Peale record with its promise of health and prosperity. It is what Bonhoeffer called *methodism*; conceiving of the gospel call as only able to be formulated in terms of a man's being down; so that you must somehow get people down, or find people who are down, in order to have them listen.

2 Corinthians 5:17

This extended parenthesis may serve as background to show that the "new creature" language of 2 Corinthians 5:17 has been charged with a freight of argumentative meaning by which the apostle would have been very surprised. It has been the primary proof text for a doctrine of where the newness of being a Christian is located, namely in the very nature of the creature. This is the meaning which, as we observed, the paraphrase by Kenneth Taylor makes even more clear, with no basis at all, in the rendering, "he is a new person *inside.*" That the *inside* is what makes a person what he or she is, is a notion of human personality which is very possible, but it is of no help with our question, and has to be brought to the text.

It is obvious that, *if* we *assume*, on the basis of our late Western personalistic culture, that "inwardness" is the most fundamental definition of what it means to be who one is, then we will feel at home reading Paul's description of the newness of the new creation as meaning a renewed inwardness. There are also non-Western and nonmodern cultures which posit such a view of the person. There is, however, nothing in the text to ratify our prior assumption that inwardness is the most fundamental level of what it means to be human, and therefore the most natural location for what it means to be renewed as human.

When Paul says that Jesus took our place, he is not talking about inwardness, but about Jerusalem. The coming of Christ was not located in the soul. His teaching was not located in the soul. His crucifixion and his resurrection were public events with witnesses. Even his ascension (which is still far harder for us as modern Western materialists to imagine) is reported as the kind of event which people who saw it could report, not reduced to what it *means* within the self-understanding of the believing person.

Then it would be more fitting, if we wish to understand the change in the creation that Paul is talking about, to assume he means not first of all an inward change from which then some outward modifications are to be derived, but a *real* change, which needs to be stated and interpreted for its own sake rather than gaining anything by being boiled down to inwardness and then expanded out from that center. So now let us dare to put the test to the Protestant claim that Scripture, when looked to afresh with a clearly defined question, can speak afresh. Does the text itself sustain such an understanding as has been sketched here?[9]

The first observation which arises from the original text is that the words *he is* are not in the text. As the use of italics in the usage of the King James Bible indicated, these two words were supplied because it was felt that they are necessary to make a meaningful sentence in English. Now there is no problem with needing to add the copulative verb "is." This is not needed as a distinct word in Greek as it is in English. Therefore to supply it adds nothing to the meaning. But the question is quite different when we ask whether the pronoun "he" had to be added, with its implied reference to the "anyone" or "someone" of the preceding clause as its antecedent. Grammatically speaking it is more proper and involves less addition to the text if we supply the copulative *without* the pronoun, and read either "creation is new" or "there is a new creation." On strictly linguistic grounds these interpretations should be attempted first before resorting to a subject drawn in from another clause.

A second consideration arises from study of the use of the noun *ktisis*, (creation) elsewhere in the New Testament. Its most frequent usage is to refer not to a thing or a creature at all, but to the act of creation, in phrases like "before the creation of the world." Its only use to refer to "human creatures" is in the context where it is not sure whether it means "humans-conceived-of-as-creatures-of-God" or "human-institutions-conceived-of-as-creatures-of-man." In either case it does not speak of individuals, but rather of categories or institutions.

Never in the New Testament is the single noun *ktisis* used to refer clearly to an individual human person perceived of as the object or the product of the creative activity of God. Since we do use the word *creature* that way in English, it is quite normal for us to consider this as one of the obvious interpretations of the passage, but we have no right to impose English connotations on a Greek text. Since the word does not have that evident meaning in the original language, we must ask what its most likely interpretation would have been for the apostle or for his readers. The most simple and literally direct interpretation which we should therefore prefer, unless there is strong argument to the contrary, is the one which takes "creation" as referring to the action whereby God makes the world. Then we should translate "if anyone is in Christ, then God creates anew." The closest to this, of the well-known translations, is the New English Bible: "there is a whole new world."

A third parallel exegetical consideration is that which comes into this text from the context. The wider context is that the apostle needs to defend his apostolic ministry, especially the way in which he has served to bring together Jews and Greeks. The immediate narrower context is his statement that he does not "know anyone after the flesh" (v. 16, KJV), that is, he does not evaluate persons according to carnal criteria ("worldly standards have ceased to count in our estimate of any man " NEB). He does not perceive people as Jew or Greek, but as the new people whom they have become in Christ. Because Christ has taken the place of all, now all persons can be seen in the image of Christ. Instead of seeing people as what they were, what their past had made them, I see them (he says) as what they became in the reconciliation worked by Christ. Consequently, I am no longer to measure, or to perceive, or to evaluate persons by the standards which I have brought with me from our fallen and divided past.

So what Paul says is not centered on the changes that take place within the constitution of the individual person, but on the changed way in which the believer is to look at the world, and especially on overcoming the "carnal standards" in which he used to perceive men in pigeonholes and categories and classes. Now he is able to perceive them in the light of their being in the place of Christ.

This view is supported by all the parallel usages. The only other use of *kainē ktisis*, "new creation," is in Galatians 6:15 where it refers to the reconciliation of Jew and Gentile. To "create one new humanity" (Eph. 2:15) is to reconcile Jew and Gentile. The "new humanity of God's creating" (Eph. 4:24) is the same; it is the unfolding of the call to unity (4:1-16) and it expresses itself in the communal virtues of telling one another the truth (4:25), working and sharing (28), edifying one another (29), and being kind (32). Thus both the "new man" and the "new creature" are, to take the texts most literally, the new community.

Still another juxtaposition of the same set of terms occurs in Colossians 3:9-11:

Do not lie to one another, since you have let yourselves be divested of the old humanity with its practices and have let yourselves be clothed with the new [humanity], which is being renewed in knowledge according to the image of its creator, where there is not Jew nor Greek. . . (my translation).

Note that the "new humanity" is defined directly as a state "where there is no Jew and Greek." When, in four quite different literary contexts (Eph. 2-3, Gal. 6, Col. 3, and our 2 Cor. 5 text), dealing with different immediate challenges in church life, we find the same themes juxtaposed:

—old and new humanity;
—no difference between Jew and Greek, slave and free;
—a distinctive new kind of knowing;
—and identification of all this with Christ himself;

we must conclude that the author is echoing a thought pattern which was frequent and fundamental in his mind.

The particular text with which we have been dealing is by no means the only one which has traditionally been read with emphasis on the inward transformation of the person. It is the one which has been used the most simply and bluntly, because it seemed to make its affirmation the most literally. Other similar texts speak of having a "new heart" (Jer. 31:31, quoted in Heb. 8:10) or of "receiving the power to become the sons of God" (John 1:12) or of being "born again" (John 3). It may then be possible to grant that the interpretation of 2 Corinthians 5:16 given above is correct and to argue that the concentration upon the transformed individual is still supported by other biblical evidence such as the texts cited above.

The intention of the above rereading is not to deny a personal or subjective or inward dimension to the experience of becoming a Christian, but to challenge the normative claim made for a view which would reduce it to only that dimension, or make that dimension the essential center.

The Constructive Alternative

If the focus is not, then, on a particular understanding of the individual standing alone and transformed alone, where does it lie?

It lies in Jesus' initial proclamation of the imminence of the kingdom. Persons must repent if they are to enter it. Repenting and entering both have about them subjective dimensions, but they can best be described in terms which include the cognitive (dealing with awareness of ideas) and the social (dealing with the awareness of other persons and groups to which one is related). The description of the change which comes over a person who repents and believes will freely include elements of emotion and self-understanding; but it will not involve any obligations to demonstrate that the changed nature is self-contained or self-interpreting or that its inwardness is prior to, or the sole and adequate cause of, or independent of, its social reality.

When we move from Jesus to Paul the answer is more clear. The reconciliation of Jew and Gentile in the "new humanity" is *first* a community event. It *cannot* happen to a lone individual. The prerequisite for personal change is a new context into which to enter. A Gentile can only find Abraham by meeting a Jew. A Jew can only celebrate the messianic age by welcoming a Gentile.

This is not to *negate* other dimensions—mental ideas, psychic self-understandings, feelings. The issue is the sovereignty of the individualistic definition over other levels of interpretation. All that is needed now is to have seen that both major texts we have tested are understood more fully and more roundly, if their location in the ethnic policy debate of the early churches is given more attention than the agenda of modern Western self-doubt.

Notes

[1] (Grand Rapids: Eerdmans, 1972).

[2] Some of these sources are cited in *The Politics of Jesus*, pp. 217-228. In addition cf. Krister Stendahl, *Paul Among Jews and Gentiles*, (Philadelphia: Fortress, 1976).

[3] This point is made by Markus Barth in "What Can a Jew Believe about Jesus . . . ?" *Journal for Ecumenical Studies*, 2 (1965):382ff., especially 395-98, but earlier and most directly by Johannes Munck, *Paul and the Salvation of Mankind*, (Richmond: John Knox, 1959), p. 87ff., and confirmed by others. The opinion of the "Judaizers," to whose criticism Paul responds, was not a representative Jewish view. They must have been making of the sign of the covenant a superstitious, ritualistic, noncovenantal use which born Jews would not have supported, and which recorded rabbinic opinion does not support. No born Jew would have given circumcision the saving value Paul has to argue against. For born Jews, the law was to be kept, but its motivation and binding character have a different framework than here. The Judaizers must then be Gentiles making a superstitious and noncovenantal ritualistic use of the covenant sign.

[4] Much recent discussion seeking to review Christian truth-claims tends to disavow the triumphal provincialism of the past, and has played the "particular"

and the "universal" over against each other. Such a formulation of the issue does violence to the New Testament witness, and is also confusing and unecumenical in our time.

⁵ James Martin in *The Last Judgment in Protestant Theology* (Grand Rapids: Eerdmans, 1963), has demonstrated how much Protestantism has changed the concept of the last judgment into a frightening prospect. According to 1 Corinthians 4:5, Paul affirms that when all secrets are revealed, "then each one will receive praise from God." (Supplied by Editor)

⁶ R. H. Strachan, *The Second Epistle of Paul to the Corinthians* (London: Hodder and Stoughton, 1935), *ad loc.*

⁷ *Ibid.*

⁸ Jean Hering, *The Second Epistle to the Corinthians* (London: Epworth Press, 1967 ET, French original published in 1958).

⁹ This section overlaps in substance with pages 217-228 of *The Politics of Jesus*. Its phrasing is independent of that text, and is derived from a draft written before it.

11

Manifestations of the Spirit of God or "Charismatic Movement"

Clarence Bauman

(1) According to Jewish life and thought, "the spirit of man is the candle of the Lord" (Prov. 20:27). This remarkable statement introduces the mystery of biblical language about the spirit in its diverse meanings, manifestations, and implications. The Hebrew word for "spirit" (*ruach*) occurs 378 times in the Old Testament with two distinct meanings: one is "wind," and refers to the atmosphere without which there is no life; the other is "breath," and presupposes the personal consciousness of the living soul. Both dimensions are mysteriously interrelated, for "when thou takest away *their* breath (*ruach*) they die and . . . when thou sendest forth *thy* spirit (*ruach*), they are created" (Ps. 104:29 f.). This duality of meaning and being is similarly conveyed by other language equivalents for "spirit" (e.g., *pneuma, anima, Geist*, etc.) and allows for some interchange of the terms and meanings: spirit "of God," "of Christ," "of holiness" (the latter occurs only three times in the O.T.). In Hebrew thought, spirit and soul are almost synonymous since the various functions and dimensions of being are not so sharply differentiated as in dichotomous or trichotomous anthropology or psychology.

These considerations raise difficult but important theological questions: On what basis and to what extent can and should we distinguish between spirit of God and spirit of man? Why should the "spirit" of God be personified more than the "will" of God or the "mind" of Christ? Why should spirit be qualified as masculine gender in English when it is feminine in Hebrew and neuter in Greek? Why should we speak of the spirit of God as a "person" existing independently of God when we do not speak of the spirit of Elijah as a person independently of Elijah?

The basic quality of spirit as breath or wind is movement. The spirit of God is always in action: whether as creation, recreation, incarnation, revelation, etc., it is always transformation by inspiration. According to Genesis 1:2, when the earth was "without form and void," the spirit (or *ruach*) of God was moving over the face of the water as the divine energy effecting and sustaining creation. Genesis 2:7 speaks of God breathing into man the breath of life (or spiriting the spirit into man), and man becoming a living being (or soul).

God's spirit is the active life-giving principle or life-force. Spirit is not inherent in the body as a property of the physical world as such, but belongs to God. Should God "take back his spirit . . . all flesh would perish" (Job 34:14, 15) for nature has no power of life on its own apart from God's spirit in it. Our life and breath is the gift or presence of the life and breath of God who knows when to give his spirit and when to take it back, and why. Life is not essentially substance but dynamic (*Kraftwirkung*) of God's will. God's spirit affects history not only physically but also morally in creating a people conformed to his will: "I will put my spirit within you, and cause you to walk in my statutes" (Ezek. 36:27). This is the meaning and ground of being of the people called Israel.

In Israel the spirit of God came suddenly, mightily, and intermittently upon certain individuals, changing their personalities and empowering or inspiring them for extraordinary tasks. Whether we think of Abraham, Moses, Jacob, Joseph, Samson, Deborah, Samuel, Saul, David, Solomon, Ezekiel, Daniel, Hosea, Amos, and so forth, Israel's patriarchs, prophets, priests, and kings were endowed with special inspiration, authority, and autonomy to give "spiritual" and political leadership. Furthermore, Jewish poets, musicians, and craftsmen claimed divine inspiration as, for example, Bezalel, of whom the Lord said to Moses (Exod. 31:3-5): "I have filled him with the spirit of God, with ability and intelligence, with knowledge and all craftsmanship, to devise artistic designs, to work in gold, silver, and bronze, in cutting stones for setting and in carving wood . . ." for the building of the tabernacle. Whether the spirit manifests itself as ecstatic "divine madness" (Hos. 9:7) or abiding restive resourcefulness (e.g., the suffering servant motif of Isaiah), the inspiration of the spirit is the perceptible but unpredictable and inscrutable manifestation of the power of God, whose reality is indisputable but whose logic remains a mystery of his will.

Throughout Jewish history, there has always been a certain tension between the dynamic autonomy of the "man of spirit" and the sacred authority of institutionalized kingship or priesthood, between the unpredictable spontaneity of the spirit and the routinization of the charisma in the cult, between the free-lance prophet who calls in question the self-evidence of the establishment and the anointed king who claims to embody God's sanction upon the political ego.

The prophets foretold the fullness of the spirit embodied in the coming Messiah of whom Isaiah says: "The spirit of the Lord shall rest upon him, the spirit of wisdom and understanding, the spirit of counsel and might, the spirit of knowledge and the fear of the Lord .... With righteousness he shall judge the poor, and decide with equity for the meek of the earth" (11:2-4a).

The birth of John, the forerunner of Jesus, was accompanied by manifestations of the spirit. According to Luke, a heavenly messenger announced to Zachariah: "Your wife Elizabeth will bear you a son and you shall call his name John ... and he will be filled with the Holy Spirit" (1:13f.). It was said of John's mother, Elizabeth, that she "was filled with the Holy Spirit" (v. 41) and that "his father Zachariah was filled with the Holy Spirit and prophesied " (v. 67).

"The child grew and became strong in spirit" (v. 80), living the ascetic life of a desert monk near the Dead Sea community of Qumran and "crying in the wilderness: Prepare the way of the Lord, make his paths straight" (Mark 1:3). To do just that, the Essenes had settled in their isolated desert commune. But John addressed his call to repentance and forgiveness to all Israel. Soon large crowds including Pharisees and Sadducees streamed out from Jerusalem to "flee the wrath to come," confessed their sins, and plunged their defiled bodies in the cleansing water of the Jordan. "As the people were in expectation, and all men questioned in their hearts concerning John, whether perhaps he were the Christ, John answered them all, 'I baptize you with water; but he who is mightier than I is coming ... he will baptize you with the Holy Spirit and with fire" (Luke 3:15-16).

(2) **Then came Jesus**—of whom it was said that he was "conceived" of the Holy Spirit (Matt. 1:20)—from Galilee to the Jordan in order to be baptized by John. "When all the people were baptized, and when Jesus also had been baptized and was praying, the heaven was opened, and the Holy Spirit descended upon him in bodily form, as a dove, and a voice came from heaven, 'Thou art my beloved Son; with thee I am well pleased' " (Luke 3:21, 22). The message of this voice from the text of Isaiah 42 contains the

confirmation: "I have put my spirit upon him" (v. 1). "Jesus, full of the Holy Spirit, returned from the Jordan, and was led by the Spirit for forty days in the wilderness. . ." (Luke 4:1 f.).

After his testing, "Jesus returned in the power of the Spirit into Galilee" (Luke 4:14), "preaching the gospel of God" (Mark 1:14), and calling disciples from the fisher folk of Galilee. On a sabbath in the synagogue at Nazareth he read from the scroll of Isaiah: "The Spirit of the Lord is upon me, because he has anointed me to preach good news to the poor . . . release to the captives . . . sight to the blind, to set at liberty those who are oppressed. . . ." Having closed the book he said: "Today this scripture has been fulfilled in your hearing" (Luke 4:18 ff.). Everywhere everyone was amazed while many were offended at his teaching, for "he taught them as one who had authority, and not as their scribes" (Matt. 7:29). "Anointed . . . with the Holy Spirit and with power . . . he went about doing good and healing all that were oppressed by the devil, for God was with him" (Acts 10:38). When Nicodemus acknowledged him to be "a teacher come from God," Jesus proceeded to instruct him in the mystery of the spiritual life saying: "Unless one is born of water and the Spirit, he cannot enter the kingdom of God. That which is born of flesh is flesh, and that which is born of the Spirit is spirit. . . . The wind blows where it wills, and you hear the sound of it, but you do not know whence it comes or whither it goes; so it is with every one who is born of the Spirit" (John 3:5-8).

After his death, Jesus reappeared to his disciples, "and while staying with them he charged them . . . to wait for the promise of the Father, which, he said, 'you heard from me, for John baptized with water, but before many days you shall be baptized with the Holy Spirit'" (Acts 1:4, 5). Just before his ascension Jesus confirmed this promise, saying to his eleven disciples: "You shall receive power when the Holy Spirit has come upon you; and you shall be my witnesses in Jerusalem and in all Judea and Samaria and to the end of the earth" (v. 8). Thereupon the disciples returned from the Mount of Olives to the Old City and "went up to the upper room, where they were staying . . . (and) devoted themselves to prayer, together with the women and Mary the mother of Jesus, and his brothers" (13, 14). About one hundred twenty persons assembled to seek God's will regarding a replacement for Judas Iscariot.

(3) "When the day of Pentecost had come" (literally "fifty" days after Passover) and the faithful throughout the diaspora flocked to Jerusalem for the harvest festival, at 9:00 a.m., as the friends of Jesus "were all together in one place . . . suddenly a sound came from heaven like the rush of a mighty wind, and it filled all the house where they were sitting. And there appeared to them tongues as of fire, distributed and resting on each one of them. And they were all filled with the Holy Spirit and began to speak in other tongues, as the Spirit gave them utterance.... At this sound the multitude came together, and they were bewildered, because each one heard them speaking in his own language . . . telling in our own tongues the mighty works of God" (Acts 2:1-4, 6, 11). Then Peter raised his voice and addressed the multitudes explaining the glossolalia happening as fulfillment of "what was spoken by the prophet Joel: 'In the last days it shall be, God declares, that I will pour out my Spirit upon all flesh, and your sons and your daughters shall prophesy...'"(2:16, 17). "And Peter said to them, 'Repent, and be baptized every one of you in the name of Jesus Christ for the forgiveness of your sins; and you shall receive the gift of the Holy Spirit.' . . . And there were added that day about three thousand souls. And they devoted themselves to the apostles' teaching and fellowship, to the breaking of bread and the prayers" (vv. 38-42).

This overwhelming outflow of energy and joy empowered the little band of timid disciples to fulfill their Master's great commission to "Go . . . and make disciples of all nations" (Matt. 28:19). Whatever we make of the accompanying language miracle (in speaking or hearing), it furthered effective communication—the very reversal of Babel. Rather than explain this happening by a modern pseudo objectivity, we need to discern its implicit meanings.

The simile "like a storm wind" is, as we have already noted, a fitting description for the phenomenon of inspiration, while the metaphor "like tongues of fire" reflects its penetrating dynamic and all-consuming passion (as the rabbis of old spoke of being surrounded by flames when absorbed in discussion of the Torah). The fire symbol reflects the prophecy of the Baptist concerning the Messiah who "will baptize you with the Holy Spirit and with fire" (Matt. 3:11), and refers to the overpowering awareness of God's self-revealed presence that totally captivates man's consciousness and wholly transforms his existence. Pentecost was the impetuous outburst of triumphant emotion of the primitive koinonia expressing the radiance of its first love and true freedom in the rapture and ecstasy of the spirit praising God and calling all men to repentance by that exercise of language which accomplished its ultimate intention of uniting men in the truth of God to know and to do his will, to proclaim righteousness and effect shalom.

There are times in the affairs of men when the spirit of God breaks in upon us "to clear the threshing floor," to gather the wheat into the granary, and to burn the chaff with unquenchable fire (Cf. Matt. 3:12). The events of that harvest festival constitute one such milestone in the chronology of *Heilsgeschichte*. From that day onwards the words and deeds of those first Christians (known as "Messianists") were endowed with that power which resists evil and overcomes the world. It is this remarkable change of mental and spiritual nature (rather than its signs of wind, fire, and language) which marks the supreme mystery and miracle of Pentecost as the birthday of the Christian Church at Jerusalem the Golden in the heart of Judaism.

(4) The Riddle of Samaria. Acts 8:14-17 speaks of people who had been baptized "in the name of the Lord Jesus" without receiving the Holy Spirit until Peter and John came up from Jerusalem and prayed for them and "laid their hands on them." These half-Gentile Samaritans had separated from the Jews in 432 B.C. to establish an independent religious community still in existence at Gerazim. After Stephen's martyrdom had triggered a general persecution of the believers in Jerusalem, they commissioned Philip, one of their seven deacons, a man full of spirit and wisdom, to preach Jesus to the Samaritans, who thereupon believed and were baptized. Why then did they not receive the spirit?

Catholics say this proves that the spirit is received only through the imposition of apostolic hands. (Which, incidentally, disqualifies John and Jesus.) Pentecostals say this proves that the spirit is always given subsequent to conversion: that sanctification follows justification as spirit baptism follows water baptism. All it "proves" is that the situation among these Samaritans was rather unstable and immature. This is exemplified by one of the "believers," Simon, a practicing magician, who sought to bribe Peter and John, hoping to purchase from them their superior spirit power. Peter roundly renounced him as being "in the gall of bitterness and in the bond of iniquity" (v. 23).

Under the circumstances it seemed fitting that an apostolic delegation from Jerusalem be sent to give further instruction and guidance to a people who for centuries had been at odds with the Jews, who, in turn, had "no dealings with the Samaritans" (John 4:9). This act of rapprochement seemed necessary lest that old schism between these two peoples rend the church from its very beginning. The unity and community that resulted in transcendence of their old differences was indeed the work and fulness of the Holy Spirit. Simon too repented of his indiscretions.

A similar incident occurred at Ephesus (Acts 19) where Paul met twelve disciples of the Baptist who had been baptized by him. Paul rebaptized them "in the name of the Lord Jesus. When Paul had laid his hands upon them, the Holy Spirit came on them; and they spoke with tongues and prophesied" (v. 5, 6).

(5) What about the Corinthian glossolalia? (1 Cor. 12-14) Some scholars have sought its origin in the pagan Bacchic celebrations with their trances and dances accompanied by ecstatic stammering and shouting in a high pitch of emotion evoked by percussion instruments (the "noisy gong" and "clanging cymbal" of chapter 13:1) creating an effect not unlike contemporary "hard rock." Others have associated the Corinthian tongues with the Delphic oracle. Rather than ascribe Christian glossolalia to pagan origins, we need to understand the symptoms of the exuberant enthusiasm of these Gentile converts in terms of the religious ideas and psychological dispositions implicit in the new faith itself.

While Paul appeared to encourage the little band of believers at Ephesus to experience a local Pentecost, at Corinth he seemed to hint at the danger of making the gift of tongues a rigid expectation of every new house-church, as if glossolalia were the primary, necessary, and inevitable evidence of the spirit of God. There is, however, no suggestion of surprise, no overtone of What's-going-on-here? in Paul's attitude. That Paul was quite familiar with this phenomenon and accepted it without reservation as a normal aspect of the Christian experience is evident from his personal testimony: "I thank God that I speak in tongues more than you all" (14:18), from his express intention: "I want you all to speak in tongues" (14:5), and from his concluding admonition: "Do not forbid speaking in tongues" (14:39). Nevertheless, Paul was concerned that this particular manifestation of the spirit be seen in perspective as one of many given "for the common good" (12:7) along with the gifts of wisdom, knowledge, faith, healing, and prophecy, for "all these are inspired by one and the same Spirit, who apportions to each one individually as he wills" (v. 11). "God has appointed in the church first apostles, second prophets, third teachers, then workers of miracles, then healers, helpers, administrators, speakers in various kinds of tongues" (v. 28). Paul notes that all do not possess the same gifts, urges that they "earnestly desire the higher gifts" (v. 31), and proceeds (in chapter 13) to "show a still more excellent way"—the way of love.

The chief problem with these "tongues," says Paul, is that they are unintelligible. This does not mean that speaking in tongues is worthless, for the person who does so may receive personal benefit as he prays, sings, or blesses "with the spirit" (14:15 f.), uttering mysteries "in the Spirit" (14:2) "with sighs too deep for words" (Rom. 8:26). "Nevertheless, in church," says Paul, "I would rather speak five words with my mind, in order to instruct others, than ten thousand words in a tongue" (14:19). The various manifestations of the spirit were intended to benefit the church, but, by this criterion, glossolalia at Corinth was found wanting for lack of interpreters endowed with the capacity to discern, and to convey to the assembly the meaning of these charismatic utterances. Paul therefore advised: "If there is no one to interpret, let each of them keep silence in the church and speak to himself and to God" (v. 28). Furthermore, Paul reminds these Corinthians that the practice of glossolalia without interpretation may invite mockery by outsiders who see in it nothing but madness (v. 23). On the other hand, an unbeliever or inquirer might well be convicted by intelligible proclamation (vv. 24, 25).

(6) Why speak in other tongues? Throughout the history of the church, many of its most charismatic leaders who initiated renewal movements owe the power of their inspiration to ecstatic manifestations of the spirit—partly due to their absorbing commitment, partly as a result of their superior intellect, and partly, perhaps, because of psychopathic tendencies. Bernard of Clairvaux (1090-1153), Hildegarde of Bingen (1098-1179), Francis of Assisi (1182-1226), Teresa of Avila (1515-1582), and even Martin Luther (1483-1546) are a very few of the world's many spiritual geniuses who reveal among the secrets of their exceptional lives extraordinary spiritual experiences. In their time the Anabaptists of the sixteenth century were known as the foremost radical spiritual enthusiasts on account of their unsuppressible contagious spiritual zeal to literally follow in the footsteps of Jesus, to be guided by his spirit, and to be his truly free and wholly faithful church. George Fox (1624-1691) frequently attested to spiritual "openings" at which he discerned quite clearly what was to be done in the power of the spirit and how the Lord's power would be over all. John Wesley (1703-1791) described invasions of the spirit at Methodist love feasts and fervent prayer meetings. Mary Campbell of the Irvingites not only spoke but also wrote in unknown tongues. Throughout all the ages of Christianity, diverse supernatural and subnormal manifestations have been identified as marks of the spirit.

Within the larger context of early Christian experience, it is not hard to appreciate the glossolalia at Corinth as a natural release of ecstatic exuberance, joyful thanksgiving, and divine adoration on the part of Gentile converts celebrating in spontaneous exultation their love of God and spiritual freedom in Christ from the dark pagan powers that hitherto blighted their fearful souls.

Today the gamut of Christian opinion on glossolalia ranges from holding speaking in tongues to be the essential initial evidence of baptism in the Holy Spirit to considering this phenomenon a very strange, unnecessary, abnormal, and possibly harmful psychic experience. In the contemporary very widespread Protestant and Catholic charismatic renewal movement, glossolalia is experienced as a natural dynamic of the Christian life. During the inspirational prayer meetings of countless new and rapidly growing charismatic communities throughout the world there is abundant nonconceptual charismatic outburst of praise and thanksgiving from the depths of the soul in a perfectly natural, controlled, but abounding and contagious manner. Its effect is freeing, edifying, and upbuilding believers, providing new strength and resilience for life in the spirit with a mounting sense of joy and a growing capacity to love and to communicate hope and meaning. These manifestations of the spirit are not strictly "useful," in a pragmatic sense, but inherently joyful and beautiful. They inspire a profound peace of the unconscious and subconscious, by which the conscious self is freed and integrated in a harmonious, resourceful, and altogether radiant way.

It is not difficult to explain charismatic religion as a reaction against the austerity of Calvinism, with its emphasis on the sovereignty of almighty God predestinating the joylessness and helplessness of unworthy man, nor to understand the charismatic enthusiasm of converts who have hitherto known only the authoritarian dominance of legalistic Catholicism or the bland repressive conformism of provincial Mennonites. The great churches have too long and too self-evidently cultivated too many meek and weak, submissive and depressed, insecure and morbid Christian stereotypes. It is no wonder that the growth of the charismatic movement is out of all proportion to that of the established churches.

Nevertheless, the history of Christendom cautions us to realize that every new emphasis on personal, spiritual experience can deteriorate to a subjective and unstable criterion of discerning the will and appropriating the grace of God. Certain traditions of Protestant pentecostalism have cultivated highly animated audience responses with ecstatic behavior patterns and emotional irregularities. Pentecostals, striving for personal holiness, tend to narrow the horizon of the world around them with the effect of walling themselves off from the rest of society. At times their belief structure has been so tensely polarized between God and Satan, good and evil, heaven and hell, that their other-worldly yearning results in a loss of reality and relevance. Sometimes these enthusiastic movements thrive under conditions of socioeconomic disruption where ecstatic religion compensates for a loss of self-image or for the inability to integrate socially or racially into the surrounding culture. Some persons attracted to pentecostalism of this type may lack an adequately structured value-attitude system, may suffer from unresolved hostilities and personal disorganization, or manifest strong affectional needs. Threatened by their own instability and lack of assurance in human relations, they seek the shelter and security of a close group identity to canalize their emotions and provide social therapy by catharsis. Some poorly integrated persons may require an intense religious experience to affect a more harmonious personality reorientation and organization.

Those who most acutely analyze the faults of the weak should realize that judging the "poor in spirit," upon whom Jesus pronounced his first blessing, is itself a pathological attempt at self-justification. Every Christian community has among its members some that are psychologically and spiritually immature or ill. It is to be expected that a charismatic community that exercises the gift of healing would, like Jesus, attract the sick. Obviously, the weak need the strong. Survival of the fittest may be the law of natural community, but the elimination of the weak is the death of spiritual community.

We need to remember that the essential mark of the spirit is not glossolalia—Jesus himself never spoke in tongues—but that "the fruit of the spirit is love, joy, peace, patience, kindness, goodness, faithfulness, gentleness and self-control" (Gal. 5:22). When the disciples of Jesus received "the Spirit of truth" (John 16:13), they were granted wisdom and strength from God to know and to do his will. The really important dimension of the invasion of the spirit lies not in ecstatic phenomena as such, but in the fact that men are endowed with higher capacities for insight, courage, and endurance, so that their very natures are conformed to the life of Jesus in such a way that God's kingdom is realized through their own inspired and inspiring lives. This experience of spiritual power manifest in freedom and love, which early Christians described as the gift or baptism of the spirit, should not be explained away in psychological or sociological terms, for the gift of that living flame, which kindled a blazing passion for personal purity and social righteousness, is the very hope and meaning of our whole being.

Postscript

a) "Except one is *born of WATER and the Spirit* he cannot enter the kingdom of God" (John 3:5).

Water is associated with cleansing, hence baptismal regeneration implies spiritual renewal (Titus 3:5). Water, the most plentiful element in our world and life, symbolized the unconscious into which the soul is immersed (Rom. 6:4, Col. 2:12) and from which it emerges reborn or recreated through the creative influence of God's spirit "over the water" (Gen. 1:2). As it "naturally" takes a lot of water to suspend the earth and sustain its life, so it "spiritually" requires a lot of water to float (or rejuvenate) the soul. Though the two factors, water and spirit, cover one reality, they are not strictly coordinate. For a self-righteous Jew to acknowledge the insufficiency of his natural birth by submitting to a baptism of repentance intended for unclean Gentiles implied a humiliation or "death" which Jesus imposed upon himself and demanded of others— though he himself baptized no one. Nevertheless, to be "born of water" symbolized the inner and outer readiness of repentant man to be endowed with God's spirit.

b) "*Where the Spirit of the Lord is, there is FREEDOM*" (2 Cor. 3:17).

All men are not naturally born free. Only those become truly free who live in "the spirit of the Lord." To become as free as God intended us to be is a tremendously big thing which lies beyond ourselves. True freedom is not a product of nature or human nature, but happens as a special act of God whereby man participates consciously and actively in the very life, breath, movement, power, word, and work of God in history. From the perspective of the Old Covenant, a living soul is one in whom the Creator breathed his own life; and from the perspective of the New Covenant, a whole person is one in whom the Redeemer inspires his own spirit. To be baptized in, filled with, or guided by the spirit of God means that God no longer exists in heavenly or theological remoteness from me, but has taken possession of me in the wholeness and fullness of my being, including my understanding, my will, my experience, and my imagination, a claim that extends to the inmost depths of the unconscious or subconscious. Whether in creation, incarnation, or inspiration, God confronts man through the life-force of his spirit, awakening him to faith, enabling him to love, and enlightening him to hope. To the extent that man is open and ready for God in the fullness of the spirit, he becomes thankful, faithful, and hopeful, that is, he becomes a responsible person.

Concretely, the spirit of the Lord frees one from that tendency of self-worship which Freud assumed to be the natural and primary condition of the ego, but which is, in effect, its grossest perversion. The healthy state is not one in which the unacceptable is suppressed or repressed into the unconscious (which then eventually becomes like the Dead Sea), but a state of spirit in which one's psychic energy flows freely outwards, inspiring cooperation with others and creating the fellowship of spirit known as church. God meant for man to be not self-centered, but altruistic, that is, to be as free to live in the world for others as God in Christ was free to live in the world for us. In fact, the whole meaning of our being his disciples lies in our becoming free to continue and complete the life and work of Jesus in that same spirit by which he was conceived or inspired. By the spirit of the Lord we are freed to reveal the word of God through our words, effect the will of God through our wills, and do the work of God through our works. But, if we compromise the adventure of this freedom of the spirit by aiming at security, we destroy ourselves, for there is no security except in choosing freedom.

c) "By this all men will know that you are my disciples *if you LOVE one another*" (John 13:35).

Love is the "more excellent way" of the spirit-filled life. Love is the primary and most distinguished fruit of the spirit (Gal. 5:22). "If I speak in the tongues of men and of angels, but have not love, I am a noisy gong or a clanging cymbal. And if I have prophetic powers, and understand all mysteries and all knowledge, and if I have all faith . . . but have not love, I am nothing. . . . Love is patient and kind; love is not jealous or boastful; it is not arrogant or rude. Love does not insist on its own way; it is not irritable or resentful; it does not rejoice at wrong, but rejoices in the right. Love bears all things, believes all things, . . . endures all things. . . . Faith, hope, (and) love abide . . . but the greatest of these is love" (1 Cor. 13:1-7, 13).

God has endowed everyone with an innate capacity to reciprocate love. But it makes a great difference in the development of a person whether he grows in trusting, loving relationships or in sinful relationships, where love is betrayed and repressed into self-love. Deprivation of love and the resulting incapacity to reciprocate love is the root of all psychic maldevelopment and mental illness. The difference between church and world (Philadelphia and Sodom) depends on how people love one another.

Human nature consists of a complex of opposing tendencies:

aggression and submission, self-assertion and self-sacrifice, independence and sociality. Too much of human interrelation resembles freezing porcupines—intermittently crowding together and separating, with quills mutually injected. Like these porcupines, we uneasily move backwards and forwards in the hope of finding the mean distance that will make life just tolerable. The *koinonia* of the spirit was meant to be God's resolution of this human dilemma. We need to learn all over again what it really means to be a fellowship of the spirit, what it means to be honest and open, to understand and to accept, to give and to forgive, to bear and to forebear, and to really love one another and be able to hope with, and for, one another. If we do this with all our hearts, there will be opened to us the full resources of the divine life as the fruit of the spirit, in faith that makes love possible, and in love that makes faith real.

d) Spiritual Guideposts

  i) "Quench not the spirit" (1 Thess. 5:19) for *the spirit is the FOUNTAIN of life.* "Rekindle the gift of God that is within you" (2 Tim. 1:6). "Do not believe every spirit" (but) "know the spirit of God" (1 John 4:1, 2). Discern the spirit of truth in the fulness of life. Respect the ways of God with men, and learn to become spiritually independent.

  ii) Pray in the spirit. Cultivate the actual presence of God in habitual silent conversation of the soul with God. Learn to dwell in reverent silence before God, "to remain open and quiet, a moist humus in the fertile darkness where the rain falls and the grain ripens—no matter how many tramp across the parade ground in whirling dust under an arid sky" (Hammarskjöld).

  iii) Keep a white book of your relations with God, a diary of your experiences of failure and of forgiveness, and so develop a design for authentic living. From time to time, plumb the depth of your soul and purify your spirit by times of profound reflection on the mystery and meaning of your being.

  iv) "Walk by the Spirit" (Gal. 5:16), "for all who are led by the Spirit of God are sons of God" (Rom. 8:14). Live by the mystery and miracle of divine guidance and "walk over the whole world answering that of God in everyman" (Fox).

Index

Index of Names

Aalen, S., 33.
Achtemeier, P., 92, 98.
Allegro, J. M., 54.
Anderson, B., 27.
Anderson, H., 98.
Amore, R., 113.

von Baer, H., 98.
Baltzer, K., 26, 27.
Baron, S., 42, 54.
Barth, M., 133.
Bender, H. S., 86.
Berrigan, D., 103ff., 110, 111, 113.
Best, E., 77, 82, 85.
Bethge, E., 104, 112.
Bigo, P., S. J., 54.
Bikerman, E., 54.
Block, L., vii.
Boelter, F., 71.
Bolkestein, H., 39, 40, 54.
Bonhoeffer, D., 101-104, 110, 111, 112, 113, 129.
Bornkamm, G., 57, 70.
Bosch, D., 96.
Braumann, G., 96, 98.
Braun, H., 112.
Bright, J., 18, 26.
Brown, S., 96.
Browning, D., 71.
Brun, L., 96.
Buber, M., 27.
Buchanan, G. W., 54, 66, 71.
Bultmann, R., 56, 70, 77, 85, 100, 105.
Bundy, W. E., 97.
Bunyan, J., 8, 15.
Burchard, C., 113.

Cadbury, H. J., 60, 61, 71.
Caird, G. B., 27, 37.
Cartledge, D., 71.
Charles, Christian L., 1.
Charles, Ellen, F. Hess, 1.
Charles, H. Raymond, 1.
Charles, Howard, vii, 1, 2, 3, 6, 7, 25, 58, 73, 84.
Charles, J. D., 1.
Charles, J. K., 1.
Charles, J. Robert, 2.
Charles, Miriam, vii, 9, 11.
Charles, Thomas, E., 2.
Chavez, C., 111.
Childs, B., 29, 30, 37, 38.
Collins, J. J., 113.
Combrink, H. J. B., 96.
Conzelmann, H., 37, 86, 112.
Cranfield, C. E. B., 77, 85.
Crockett, L. C., 54, 97.
Crossan, J. D., 70, 71.

Dahood, M., 37.
Dale, R. W., 16.
Dalman, G., 97.
Darwin, C., 70.
Daube, D., 36.
Davies, J. H., 98.
Degenhardt, H. J., 54.
Deissmann, A., 100, 112.
Detweiler, R., 84.
Dihle, A. 112.
Dodd, C. H., 4.
Doty, W., 84.
Duhm, B., 17.
Dungan, D. L., 71.
Durkheim, E., 70.

148

Edwards, G., 29, 37.
Eichrodt, W., 37.
Eller, V. 86.
Eltester, W., 97, 98.
Erikson, E., 63, 69, 71.

Farrar, F., 92, 98.
Farrer, A. M., 81, 86.
Flusser, D., 54, 70, 71, 98.
Foerster, W., 113.
Ford, J. M., 37.
Frank, T., 54.
Freedman, D. N., 26, 27.
Freud, S., 63, 70, 146.
Frey, H., 35, 37.
Fuller, R. H., 114.

Gaechter, P., 54.
Gelin, A., 54.
George, A., 97, 98.
Gettys, J., 84.
Gilula, M., 27.
Godet, F., 92, 98.
Goulder, M., 72.
Gourbillon, J. G., 55.
Granskou, D., 71.
Greehy, J. G., 55.
Guilding, A., 97.
Güttgemanns, E., 84.

Haas, H., 113.
Habel, N., 26, 27.
Haenchen, E., 98.
Hammarskjöld, D., 147.
Harnack, A., 101.
Harrelson, W., 26, 27.
Harrisville, R., 113, 114.
Heichelheim, F. M., 54.
Hengel, M., 54.
Hering, J., 122, 134.
Hermission, H. J., 113.
Hick, J., 72.
Hilebrand, P., viii.
Hill, D., 96.
Hitler, A., 102.
Hobbs. E. C., 80, 81, 86.
Hoffmann, P., 113.
Holladay, W., 26.
Holtz, T. C., 113.
Horst, A. S., 1.
van der Horst, P., 113.
Hyatt, P., 27.
Hyldahl, N., 97.

Jägerstätter, F., 111.
James, W., 11.
Janzen, W., 36.
Jeremias, J., 54, 70, 71, 88, 96.
Johnson, R., 70.
Jönsson, J., 62, 71.
Jung, C. G., 63.
Juschke, A., 55.

Kandler, H. J., 55.
Karli, Henry, 1.
Karli, Peter, 1.
Keck, L., 45, 54, 57, 70, 92, 98.
Kelber, W., 78, 79, 80, 85, 86.
Keller, H., 11.
King, M. L., 102ff., 110.
Koester, H., 112.
Konrad, J. F., 114.
Kopp, C., 97.
Kramer, S. N., 27.
Kraus, H. J., 27.
Kuhn, G., 29, 37.
Kuist, H. T., 4, 10, 83, 84.
Kundsin, K., 70.
Kutsch, E., 26.

Lambert, W. G., 113.
Lampe, G. E. H., 98.
Larsson, E., 86.
Leaney, A. R. C., 55, 98.
Lee, R. S., 66, 71.
Legasse, S., 55.
Lehman, C. K., 8.
Lightfoot, J. B., 14.
Lightfoot, R. H., 97.
Lind, M., vii, 28.
Linnemann, E., 71.
Lohfink, G., 96.
Lührmann, D., 112.
Luz, U., 77, 79, 85, 86.

McCasland, V., 86.
Machoveč, M., 56, 70.
Macintosh, H. R., 15.
McIntyre, J., 57, 70.
Martin, J., 134.
Marx, K., 70.
Masson, C., 98.
Matthiae, K., 84.
Mazlish, B., 70.
Mendelsohn, I., 27.
Metzger, B. M., 97.
Michaelis, W., 77, 85, 86.
Mill, J. S., 70.

Miller, M. H., 98.
Minear, P., 112.
Moffatt, J., 118ff.
Müller, H. P., 29, 30, 36, 37.
Munck, J., 133.
Myers, J. M., 27.

Nicklesburg, G. W., 113.
Nissen, A., 112.
Nixon, R., 103ff.
Noack, B., 55.
Noth, M., 25, 27, 28.

O'Collins, G., 63, 68, 70, 71.
Oepke, A., 86.
van Oyen, H., 112.

Patte, D., 84.
Peale, N. V., 129.
Perrin, N., 74, 77, 84, 85.
Petersen, N. R., 84.
Philonenko, M., 113.
Phipps, W., 67, 71.
Piper, J., 114.
Plummer, A., 92, 97, 98.
Polzin, R. M., 84.
Potterie, I., 98.
Preuss, H. D., 28.
Prevallet, E. M., 91, 97, 98.

Quesnell, Q., 75, 84.

von Rad, G., 28.
Reimarus, H. S., 70.
Reimer, L., vii.
Rendtorff, R., 26, 99.
Rengstorf, K. H., 86.
Reploh, K. G., 78, 85.
Repo, E., 81, 86.
Richter, W., 22, 27.
Rigaux, B., 77, 85.
Ristow, H., 84.
Robinson, J., 116.
Robinson, W. C., Jr., 98.
Ross, J. F., 27.
Rostovtzeff, M., 54.
Rudolph, W., 26.
Rusche, H., 55.

Safrai, S., 54, 55.
Samain, E., 98.
Sanders, J., 96.
Schlatter, A., 97.
Schmid, J., 97, 98.
Schmidt, K. L., 77, 85, 97.
Schneider, G., 104, 106, 109, 112.

Schottroff, L., 112, 113, 114.
Schreiber, J., 75, 78, 79, 84, 85.
Schulz, P. A., 55.
Schürer, E., 55.
Schürmann, H., 96, 97, 98.
Schweitzer, A., 70.
Schweizer, E., 77, 85, 113.
Skinner, J., 26.
Smith, M., 113.
Smith, R. H., 35, 37.
Speiser, E. A., 27.
Stein, R., 85.
Stendahl, K., 133.
Stern, M., 54, 55.
Stöger, A., 55.
Strachan, R. H., 122, 134.
Strecker, G., 74, 84, 98.

Talbert, C., 70.
Taylor, K., 129.
Taylor, V., 77, 85.
Tcherikover, V., 54.
Tolbert, M., 96.
Traina, R., 73.
Trocme, E., 57, 61, 70, 71.
Tröltsch, E., 28.
Trueblood, E., 71.

van Unnik, W. C., 112.

Vermes, G., 70.
Via, D., 84.
Vielhauer, P., 74, 84.
Violet, B., 97.
Voss, G., 97.

Walter, N., 55.
Weiser, A., 26.
Weiss, K., 74, 75, 78, 84, 85.
Wellhausen, J., 26.
Westcott, B. F., 16.
White, W. W., 16.
Wilckens, U., 98.
Williams, J. G., 26.
Wilson, R. D., 3.
Wilson, S. G., 96.
Windisch, H., 79, 85.
Wright, G. E., 26.

Yadin, Y., 54.
Yoder, J. H., vii, 86.
Yoder, P. B., 84.

Zahn, G., 113.
Ziener, G., 29, 37, 38.
Ziesler, J. A., 80, 86.

Scripture Index

Genesis
1:2	136, 145
1:3	30
2:7	136
17:9-14	12
39:4	18
41:34	18

Exodus
1-24	25
3:2-3	27
3:8	24
3:9	24
3:10	24
3:11	24
3:12	24
3:16	24
3:16-17	24
3:17	24
4:1	24
4:2-9	24
4:10-12	24
4:13	24
7:5	37
7:9	30
7:17	37
7:19	30
8:12	30
8:22	37
9:9	30
9:22	30
10:1f.	35
10:15	31
10:21	30, 37
10:21-29	29, 37
10:27	34
10:27ff.	31
10:28ff.	30
11:1-12:36	30
12:12	37
14:4, 18	37
23:11	49
23:20	79, 81
23:23-33	80
24-32	80
24:1, 9	80
24:12, 15	80
24:16	80
25:9	80
31:3-5	136
33:1-3	80
34:29-35	80

Leviticus
19:9-10	49
19:18	105, 106
23:22	49
24:13, 14, 23	90
24:14, 23	92
25:6	49

Numbers
15:35, 36	90, 92
23	81
33:4	37

Deuteronomy
1:1-5	80
1:8	79
4:1	79
6:18	79
13:1-11	92
14:28-29	49
15:1-2	49
16:11	49
16:20	79
23:1	113
24	80
24:19-22	49
26:12-15	49
28:29f.	33

Joshua
5:10-15	81
10:18	18

Judges
6-8	27
6:11b-17	22
6:12	21
6:14, 15	21
6:25-32	22
8:2	49
8:22	21
8:22ff.	23
9:1-57	22

Ruth
2	49

1 Samuel
8:7	23
8:22	22
9-10:16	22

2 Kings
6:15-23	107

23:1-25　　19
25:22　　　18

1 Chronicles
26:32　　　18

Nehemiah
8:10　　　49

Tobit
4:15　　　106

Esther
9:22　　　49

2 Maccabees
3:4ff.　　40

Job
28:12-17　40
34:14, 15　136

Psalms
91:11, 12　93
104:29f.　　135
105　　　36
105:28　　31
105:28-36　31, 33

Proverbs
20:27　　　135
25　　　113
25:21　　　107

Book of Wisdom
17:1f.　　33
17:21　　33

Isaiah
8:22-9:2　33
11:2-4a　137
13:9ff.　31
24:13　　49
40:3　　79, 81
42　　　137
42:1　　138
43:18ff.　vii
43:18-19　112
58:6　　92
60:1-3　33, 34
60:2　　33
61　　　96
61:1, 2　92
61:2　　88

Jeremiah
1　　　20
1:4-5　　27
1:9-10　　17
1:10　　18
1:13ff.　26
1:15　　19
3:6-10　　19
4:1-2　　20
4:23　　32
12:14-17　20
22:15-16　19
23:5-6　　19
25:9　　26
26　　　20
26:12　　20
26:15　　20
26:16　　21
26:17ff.　21
26:18　　21
27:6　　19, 26
28:8　　21
31　　　20
31:31　　132
31:31-34　20
33:14-18　19
40:11　　18
43:10　　26
51:59ff.　19

Ezekiel
30:17　　32
30:18ff.　32
32:7ff.　　32
36:27　　136

Daniel
5:3　　106

Hosea
9:7　　136
12:13　　28

Joel
2:31　　32
3:14f.　　32

Amos
8:9　　31
9　　　31

Micah
7:1　　49

OF JESUS

Nahum
1:8　　　　32

Zephaniah
1:14f.　　　31

Malachi
3:1　　　　79, 81
3:10　　　　49

Matthew
1:20　　　　137
3:11　　　　139
3:12　　　　140
4:5　　　　91
4:5-7　　　91
4:6　　　　91, 93
5:9　　　　111
5:11　　　　90
5:45　　　　61
7:11　　　　61
7:29　　　　138
8:7　　　　94
10:14　　　93
11:5　　　　58
13:24-30　　60, 65
13:45f.　　60, 65
13:55　　　64
18:12-14　　65
18:23ff.　　59
18:23-35　　60, 62, 65
20:1-16　　58, 59, 65
20:12　　　59
20:17b　　　75
20:25-27　　25
20:30　　　75
21:31　　　59
24:29f.　　35
24:45-51　　65
25:14-30　　59, 60, 65
28:19　　　139

Mark
1:1　　　　79
1:2, 3　　74, 75
1:3　　　　137
1:11　　　　68
1:14　　　　138
1:14f.　　　58
1:35　　　　94
1:45　　　　93
2:12　　　　89
2:15　　　　64
2:17　　　　58

2:23　　　　75
3:6　　　　89
3:19b　　　64
3:29, 35　　75
3:34f.　　　68
4:4, 15　　75
4:17　　　　96
6:1-6a　　　96
6:2　　　　89
6:2, 3, 6　　89
6:3　　　　64, 65, 89, 90
6:6a　　　　89
6:7-8:21　　76
6:8　　　　75
6:12, 13　　93
6:30-8:21　　85
6:30-8:26　　75
6:52　　　　85
7:24　　　　81
8:3　　　　75
8:14-21　　85
8:21　　　　76
8:22-26　　85
8:27　　　　75, 76, 77, 78, 80, 83
8:27-30　　81, 82, 85
8:27-10:52　　74, 75, 76, 77, 78, 79,
　　　　　　80, 81, 82, 83, 86
8:29, 32　　82
8:31　　　　74
8:31, 33, 34　82
8:31-38　　81, 82
8:32-33　　74
8:34　　　　77, 83
8:34ff.　　　77
8:34-38　　74
9　　　　　80
9:1　　　　80
9:1-29　　81, 82
9:1, 43, 45　　78
9:2　　　　80
9:2, 3　　　80
9:2, 7　　　80
9:5　　　　80
9:7　　　　80
9:19　　　　80
9:30-41　　81, 82
9:31　　　　74
9:32　　　　74
9:33　　　　78
9:33, 34　　75, 76, 77, 80
9:33-37　　82
9:35-37　　74
9:42-50　　81
9:43, 45, 47　80

9:43-10:31	82	3:1-4:30	98
9:47	78	3:15-16	137
10	80	3:21, 22	137
10:1	81	3:23	63
10:1-12	80, 81, 82	4	96, 97
10:2-12	80	4:1f.	138
10:13-31	81	4:9	91
10:14	78	4:9-12	91
10:15	68	4:10, 11	93
10:15, 23, 24, 25	78	4:12	93
10:17	76	4:14	138
10:17-22	82	4:14-30	96, 97
10:17, 32, 46, 52	75	4:16-22	96
10:18	63	4:16-30	87, 96, 97, 98
10:27	83	4:16, 20	90
10:32	75, 76, 77, 78	4:18	88
10:32-45	81, 82	4:18, 19	87, 92
10:32f.	74	4:18ff.	138
10:35-41	74	4:19	88
10:35-45	82	4:21	87, 88
10:42-45	74	4:22	89
10:43-44	25	4:22ab	87, 88
10:45	83	4:22c	87
10:46a	81	4:23	87, 88
10:46c	75, 76	4:23a	89
10:46-52	81, 82	4:24	87, 88, 92, 96
10:46, 52	77	4:25-27	87, 88, 89, 92
10:52	76, 77	4:25-29	96
11:1	94	4:28	87, 89, 90, 96
11:8	75, 94	4:28, 29	92, 95
11:10	78	4:28-30	95
12	106	4:29	90, 93, 97
12:8	90	4:29a	87, 90
12:14	75	4:29b	87
12:32	106	4:29-30	92
13:24ff.	34	4:30	87, 92, 93, 94, 95, 97, 98
14:21	94	4:31	95
14:27, 29	96	4:42	94
14:29	94	4:43	95
14:53	91	5:12-14	93
15:1	91	5:15	93
15:20	91	5:26	89
15:27	91	6:11	89
		6:22	90
Luke		6:32-35	112
1:13f.	137	6:36	58
1:15, 41, 67	89	6:47-49	66
1:41	137	7:1-10	96
1:67	137	7:6	94
1:68, 78	88	7:11	94
1:80	137	7:16	88
2:7	64	7:41-43	58
2:41	94	8:13	96
2:52	63	9:6	93, 95

9:43	96	22:25-27	25
9:51	93, 94, 95, 98	22:31-34	96
9:51, 53	95	22:33	94
9:52	88, 94	22:51	98
9:53	94	22:54	91
9:56, 57	94	22:66	91
10:5	111	23:1	91
10:6	111	23:26	91
10:12, 13-16	96	23:32	91
10:29-37	59, 60, 65	23:34	90
10:38	94	23:44f.	35
11:5-8	62	23:46	90
11:5ff.	61	24:13	94
11:7	68	24:13-15, 28	95
11:20	58	24:26	98
11:29-32, 33	96	24:26, 27, 44-46	91
12:42-46	59	24:28	94
13:18-21, 28	96	24:47	96
13:18f.	61		
13:22	94	**John**	
13:31-33	93	1:12	132
13:33	94, 95	3	132
14:16-24	62	3:5	145
14:16ff.	59	3:5-8	138
14:25	98	4:9	140
14:28	66	7:30, 44	93
15:4-7	60	8	97
15:4-32	58	8:20	93
15:8-10	66, 67	8:59	92, 97
15:11-32	59, 65	9	97
15:31	62	9:1-41	37
16:1-9a	60, 65	9:39	35
16:3	62	12:36	35
16:19-31	60	12:36b, 37	35
17:11	88, 93, 94, 95	13:34	100
18:1-8	62, 66, 67	13:35	146
18:6f.	61	16:13	144
18:9-13	59	17:3	14
18:11	62		
18:31	91	**Acts**	
18:31, 35	98	1:4, 5	138
18:35	75	1:8	138
19:1	93	1:10, 11	95
19:1, 28	95	1:11	95
19:1, 45	98	1:13, 14	138
19:11	98	2:1-4, 6, 11	139
19:28	94	2:4	89
19:28-36	94	2:16, 17	139
19:29, 41	98	2:38-42	139
19:36	94	3:10	89
19:44	88	3:15	83
20:9-19	90, 96	4:8, 31	89
21:25	35	5:17	89
22:22	94	5:20	95

5:31	83	**1 Corinthians**	
7:54-60	90	4:5	134
7:58	92	12-14	141
7:58a	90	12:7	141
7:59	90	12:11	141
7:60	90	12:28	141
8:4, 40	94	12:31	141
8:14-17	140	13	141
8:23	140	13:1	141
8:26, 27, 36	95	13:1-7, 13	146
9:11, 15, 31	95	14:2	142
9:17	89	14:5	141
9:32, 38	94	14:15f.	142
10:20	95	14:18	141
10:38	93, 138	14:19	142
11:19	94	14:23	142
12:7, 10	98	14:24, 25	142
12:10	94	14:28	142
12:17	95	14:39	141
13:6, 14	94		
13:9	89	**2 Corinthians**	
13:45	89	3:17	145
13:50	90	5	116, 117, 118, 132
14:14-52	96	5:11	121
14:19	96	5:11-15	119
14:24	94	5:12	121
15:3, 41	94	5:13	121
16:6	94	5:14	121, 122
16:7, 16	95	5:15	121
16:26	98	5:16	131, 132
17:14	95	5:17	123, 129
17:23	94	8:9	66
18:6	95		
18:23, 27	94	**Galatians**	
19:1, 21	94	1:8, 9	105
19:5, 6	141	1:10	120
19:21	95	5:12	105
19:23ff.	89	5:16	147
19:28	89	5:22	144, 146
19:29	89	6	132
20:1, 22	95	6:15	131
20:2, 25	94		
20:25	94	**Ephesians**	
21:5	95	2-3	132
22:10, 21	95	2:15	131
23:3	105	4:1-16	131
28:26	95	4:24	131
28:30, 31	95	4:25	132
		4:28	132
Romans		4:29	132
6:4	145	4:32	132
8:14	147		
8:26	142	**Philippians**	
		3:2	105

OF JESUS

Colossians
1:15	3
1:15-20	3
1:20	111
2:12	145
3	132
3:9-11	132

1 Thessalonians
5:19	147

1 Timothy
1:15	69

2 Timothy
1:6	147

Titus
3:5	145

Hebrews
2:10	83
5:8	63
8:10	132
11:8	7
11:8-10	86
12:2	83

1 John
2:8-11	101
4:1, 2	147

Revelation
6:12	34
8:12	34
8:13	34
16:10	34
16:11	34

Chapter 5
Sirach
3:30	43
4:1-5	43
4:8	43
4:10	43
5:1-2	42
6:14	43
6:17	41
7:10	43
7:22	41
7:32-40	43
9:16	41
10:27, 30	41
11:4	42
11:9	41
11:10-11	42
11:12-23	43
11:22	43
11:23-27	42
12:3-7	43
12:14	41
13:3-8	42
13:15-17	43
13-18	43
13:21-29	42
13:23	41
14:11-17	41
18:15-18	43
18:25	42
21:8	42
22:23	43
27:2	42
28:25	41
29:1-10	43
29:8-17	43
29:14-26	42
29:21-22	41
31:8-10	42
31:12-31	41
32:1-13	41
33:20-24	41
33 [G 30] 27	40
34:21-26	43
40:17	41
42:1-7	42

Qumran documents
1 QM
1 QM 5:4-6	44
1 QM 5:7	44
1 QM 5:11-14	44
1 QM 6:11	44

1 QS
1 QS 5:2	45
1 QS 5:14-20	45
1 QS 6:6	45
1 QS 6:19	45
1 QS 6:22	45
1 QS 6:24	45
1 QS 8:22	45
9:7-9	45

CD
CD 6:15-17   44
CD 6:20   45
CD 8:5   44
CD 10:18   45
CD 12:6-11   44
CD 13:14-16   45
CD 19 [1] 9-10 44
CD 20 [2] 7   45